To Ken + Linda, with all best wishes

PEACE ETC.

(a journey through open heart surgery and other scary

things, written to lessen your anxiety, whatever it may be)

by

BOB BEVERLEY

Bob Beverley

photography by

DAVID SPAGNOLO

JULIE SPAGNOLO

The author would like to introduce to you the music of Marian Grudko.

"Come What May," an excerpt from Marian's musical tale, "Dragonfly Bog," is one of the most peace-inducing works I have ever heard. You can listen to it on her website, marriangrudko.com.

Designed and produced by Elliot Toman
www.asubtleweb.com

ISBN 978-1500630706

This book is dedicated

to

THE CARDIOTHORACIC TEAM

at

VASSAR BROTHERS MEDICAL CENTER

POUGHKEEPSIE, NEW YORK, U.SA.

THE JOURNEY

PREFACE

i hope this book helps you to be less afraid, more peaceful and content and brave

when i was young i didn't even know i was anxious

it was home turf

fish don't discover water

i have done all kinds of things, thought all kinds of things, to lessen my anxiety, and i tell you many of these things in the following pages

it is written with the conviction that we need all the help we can get

three things to note. i am a psychotherapist, so these pages will reflect the immense privilege of my vocation, that of walking with people through the depth of human struggle and fear towards growth and peace of mind. i also happen to be a christian, and so the following pages draw on that tradition. i work hard to be a sane person of faith, so please let me know if there is anything written here that is not universally applicable, or off-putting in any way, even if it is half a sentence

thirdly and ironically, as you'll discover, these pages were written during a sudden onslaught of severe back pain and the startling news that my heart had developed severe aortic valve regurgitation and an ascending aortic aneurysm, things which do not make for peace, things which make for open heart surgery

and so this book will be more autobiographical than intended, with my heart as the peace lab, in more ways than one

these reflections on peace were written as part of my weekly blog called "The Dig" and for some reason during that time i decided not to capitalize most words and to avoid most periods and a lot of other punctuation. this helped my writing flow so i kept with the format, imagining also that the little words symbolized the fact that peace is composed of many little good things

this is not light stuff. so take your time as you read, and appreciate with me the beautiful, peace-inducing photography of David and Julie Spagnolo. i am honored that both these artists brought their talent to this book.

i am grateful to all who have helped me in days gone by and in recent days when the waters got rough. i am deeply indebted to the cardiothoracic team at the Vassar Brothers Medical Center, for saving my

PEACE ETC.

life and for offering personal, community focused, world class care to the Hudson valley; and so i have dedicated this book to them

actions speak louder than words, so they say, and so fifty per cent of the profit from this book will go to Vassar Brothers Medical Center, to help people less fortunate than you or I

love. respect. gratitude. peace.

bob beverley

THE GREAT TEACHER

my bed has turned into a hammock lately and one of the consequences is that i have had about twenty two thousand muscle spasms, some of them accompanied by terrible screams as lightning bolts of pain have danced on my back and shown me, for the first time, that something in my body is faster than an olympic athlete

i mean these muscle spasms are very talented, they move at lightning speed, back and forth, back and forth, all the while grabbing my back with a vice like grip that captures my attention better than any marketing expert in the world

i hope that my screams have not disturbed your sleep, as they have mine

pain is the great teacher and so now i am dedicated to getting a new bed and purchasing a new back somewhere

when i lie in bed i think of you, i think of the world you live in, the peace you have, the peace you don't have, and i yearn for you to know that there is nothing that brings peace like dedicating yourself to the desperately needed relief of human pain, yours and others

the trouble with pain and fear is that, for the moment, perhaps longer, it makes us legitimately self-centered, so acutely absorbed by ragged pain, the coming crash, the impending doom

nobody with permanent migraines saves the world

(this isn't really self-centered, it is having a self that needs to take care of a migraine)

who can sing "here comes the sun, little darling" when we hear the hoof beats of the four horsemen of the apocalypse?

however

after a while, we can get so used to suffering that we don't do much about it and our dedication to even the relief of our own suffering gets put on the back burner as we are swamped with the obligations of life, there are bills to pay, jobs we must attend, things we have to clean up, so much we have to fix, another funeral to go to

we are swept along by habit, we are constrained, and the way our lives are set up becomes a straitjacket so that we move in accustomed ways, and we can't see a new way, we can't do a new way, we are more unconscious than we know, we are in a spell, a witches brew of habit and fear and so used to it pain this is the human condition

and it's nowhere near all your fault

at the end of his book, "monkey mind," daniel smith tells us that he now realizes that so much of his fear has only been in his head and so he ends the book with the sentence "i am a fool" and this made me sad for him, very sad, so if you know him will you tell him that he is not a fool, will you tell him "what, did you go down in the basement and pick your mother who you say was the monkey of fear who raised you, did you go down in your basement and build the human brain that is so susceptible to anxiety, did you with nail and hammer construct "the heartache and the thousand natural shocks that flesh is heir to?"

oh yes, we are foolish in some ways, we are to blame at times, but i have met thousands of people whose superego is so accusatory, so relentlessly punishing, so talented, so 24/7, that they hardly have a moment's peace and these are good people, salt of the earth people, the ones who get told "you are beating yourself up too much" but the truth is they are not beating themselves up, their superego is just sending constant muscle spasms their way, you should have done this, you should have done that

people need salvation, blessing, soothing, grace, touch, and affirmations in abundance

we don't need 207 pairs of shoes

we don't need all the stuff, that ultimately constrains us

again, this is not all our fault

we are seduced by the allure of capitalism and we feel "i am somebody" as we check our iPhone or sit in our massive library or drive around in our hot car

we're in another spell, enchanted by stuff

how hard to see we were enchanting when we arrived naked in the world, and are now more enchanting than a pair of shoes or a chrysler 300

how hard to think, to think through, to ask what works, what satisfies, what will really bring peace

nothing brings peace like dedicating yourself to the desperately needed relief of human pain, yours and others

WARNINGS

IN HONOR OF DR. ANDREW CHERNACK, MY INTERNIST

the human brain is very weird, and so is everything when you think about it. an alien landing from some-where beyond where the hubble can see, would find ants and bananas and a cell phone very odd and amusing, if not riveting to see for the first time

the human brain might take the weirdness cake, though, not only in terms of its dreams and fantasies and astounding computing ability, but also how it processes anxiety

i know a young man who almost made the u.s. ski team, which means that he can go so fast down a mountain that just watching him would put us mortals into a mile long panic attack. he is scared to climb a twelve foot ladder

one of my friends could go fishing in the early morning in a fog on the long island sound and sit there calmly waiting for a fish to bite, but could not get up the courage to take a shower in his own bathroom in the afternoon.   morning showers were doable

i can give a talk before a thousand people and be far more peaceful than if you asked me to change your tire and then stood there watching me

it is easier to be peaceful once you get the leverage of our common, human oddness. it gives us a bit of distance from the looming presence of fear, which acts like it is the king of truth and perspective and sanity

it also helps when we share our common propensity to fear and don't act like the king or queen of nothing bothers me

likewise, when our fear or pain is simply acknowledged, as opposed to quickly explained away, that too is soothing and bracing. when i told my bni (business networking international) colleagues about my surgery, a very bright woman named carol, who was aware of all the injuries i have sustained throughout my life, put her hand on my shoulder, shook her head, and said "you poor man!" i found that to be one of the most comforting things that anyone said to me during my recent adventure under the knife

of course, the biggest truth is that we need so much said to us and for us, so much done for us, because we don't want to walk a lonesome valley, don't want to walk it by our self

peace is a community project

peace is the gift of love

fear also has its chorus and fear making has its devotees

there are many legitimate things to fear in this world and the best thing we can do about that is to live wisely and healthfully, stay away from the things that rightfully scare us, and don't go where it isn't safe, unless that is your business (military, police, etc.)

don't text and drive

eat your salads and fruits and vegetables

don't swim with anacondas

no holy book says that any of us are an exception to the rules, so do allow the light to inform your driving habits, your ability to overdo it, and any notion you have that sword play is not real

"those who live by the sword, die by the sword" whether that sword be a drone bomb, a punch, or a barrage of contemptuous advice

the thing you feel most when you get stretchered into the lonesome valley they call an operating room, or when you lie in bed coming in and out of consciousness, unable to speak because you are intubated, which means tubes down your throat, is that pain is very real and yet so, so much of our pain is unnecessary, so insane, so heartless, so much of a waste of time

so much of an insult to the sheer gift of life, the gift of a body, the gift of one another

and yet i know that those forced to see their children eat grass to survive are tempted to pick up the sword, as would i

peace is a community project

peace is the gift of love and respect to each other

fear is a chorus inside us

there are skilled, persistent scouts in our brain that will find things to fear, create things out of nothing, and imagine trouble where there is no trouble

the human brain is a neurotic place, whose neurosis becomes second nature can any nurse comprehend that while they are checking the bags of drugs connected to your arm and simultaneously looking at your monitor, that you are looking in their eyes for that sign which indicates your vitals are dropping and that he or she is about to call a "code blue?"

shouldn't hospitals inform incoming patients that you should work hard at remembering your room number because when they call a code blue in the middle of the night you wonder if your room is the one they just mentioned for all the hospital to hear?

shouldn't someone warn you that the machines make all kinds of noises and that you should simply ignore them until a professional at medical sounds comes in and tells you "it is now time to worry"

instead, the nurses smile and walk peacefully to the neurotic in the next room, the marching troupe of code warriors walk back to their stations, and the machines keep beeping while you are urged to get some rest

we need to find, in hospitals and elsewhere, experts whom we trust implicitly, experts who let us know that the scouts in our brain are more often than not, monkeys swinging from vine to vine, making up trouble, not out of thin air (for the bags, monitors, codes, and beeps are real), but they make needless trouble nonetheless, for true trouble is quite capable of making itself known very clearly and very loudly

become an expert at facing true trouble and your soul will grow in strength and wisdom, and you will have more peace

this means that peace is not an every moment reality

when we hear trouble or spot trouble or are told we are in trouble, we are not always calm and serene

a few months ago, my internist dr. andrew chernack told me that my aortic valve was making more noise than usual and that i should schedule an echocardiogram

i put this on a bit of a back burner because, at the time, i was experiencing that severe back pain, and not being able to lie down made it very excusable to put off the procedure

the next time i saw dr. chernack my back was quite a bit better, and so i was hoping that my aorta had calmed down because of less pain, and that i could postpone any possible further troubling reality till a more convenient time, which would be never

while he was listening to my heart, i mumbled some wishful thinking about giving myself a break, since i had been through so much lately, and he interrupted me and said "go get the damn echo" this did not make me calm and serene

i did not like him at that moment, because i wanted a reassuring, peaceful comment like "sure, take your time, easy does it"

it is quite likely that his assertiveness saved my life, because i could have walked around in a fog of an "all is well" no back pain existence, biding my time, not knowing that an ascending aortic aneurism was part of my inner body shenanigans, something that could quickly lead to the end of all my troubles

sometimes people who hurt our feelings save our life

my therapist called this "feeling worse and doing better"

sometimes peace comes only after we face and deal with necessary trouble

in this weird world, trouble and peace can walk hand in hand to a better place

CONTROL

IN HONOR OF DR. GARY NATHANSON, MY CARDIOLOGIST

it is a wonder we can have a moment's peace

for example, i had a heart to heart talk with my cardiologist on march 3, 2014 and i decided later that it was not a heart to heart talk

as is appropriate and understandable, his heart was in his chest calmly beating and pumping out a prestigious amount of blood for his very own self, and he was very much in his head telling me all the factual details about my rather precarious heart and what i needed to do about it

in other words, it was a head to heart talk, his head, my heart

this would explain why he could later send me a letter about our meeting and mention that he had gone over the risks in detail

"risks that include but are not limited to death, MI, CVA, renal failure, arrhythmia, infection, bleeding. The patient understands these risks and agrees to proceed."

you gotta love the "not limited to death" part

i wonder what the word "understands" means when your mind, without your conscious volition, has already decided to check out and head to pluto or mars

i wonder what "agrees to proceed " means when your heart is in your throat and seems to be pumping emotional fog into your brain by the second as you gamely try to appear rational and focused while your brain is screaming "beam me up, scotty" and your mouth is tempted to do its own rendition of edvard munch's "the scream"

after all, let's look at the letters, none of which i recall hearing in our mind to heart talk

MI equals myocardial infarction which is a fancy word for what billy joel sings about when he rattles off "heart attack ack ack" but not even billy joel can put me in a singing mood when it comes to my own personal, possible MI

if you look up CVA on wikipedia it can mean "contextual value added" in education,
credit value adjustment in economics, the christian vegetarian association in religion, or it is a symbol for attack aircraft carriers in the military. alas, not even your fear filled eyes can escape the point in wiki

where the scholars say CVA can also mean "cerebrovascular accident" in medicine, which they kindly mention is "also known as stroke"

i think i will go with the christian vegetarian association, that will be good for my heart

jesus and kale and broccoli and me, what a quartet

a long time ago one of my therapy supervisors told me to advise others and myself, when in severe overload, to "look away from the pain, look away from the fear"

disassociate, baby, disassociate

look away

it is a necessary tool for peace

do not be ashamed of it

use it

but some things in life, like the doctor's letter, make it hard to look away, and i am surprised that they don't send letters of this kind with a package of gummy bears and some stickers and a carton of cigarettes and some onion rings for comfort food and the warning that this kind of letter or discussion can cause anal failure

that seems much more likely than renal failure, whatever that is

(i am not looking anything else up)

or how come doctors don't have this kind of discussion or send this kind of letter without some of the accompanying medical marijuana we have been hearing about

or at least meet me in the office with a gin and tonic, on the house, or let health insurance fully cover it and tell the whole world, hippa shoved rudely aside, that my doctor sat down man to man with me and we had a toast to my health, my initiation into the christian vegetarian association, and my long trip on 'starship enterprise" where i will travel to a place where there is no need to scream and no open heart surgery

beam me up, scotty

i think if my grandson, victor, were having a mind to mind talk with the doctor he would have anal failure all over his organized medical office, just to let the universe know that this is no fair way to run the universe, and he is going to even the score a bit and get somebody else's blood pressure heading upwards with an all out military attack, CVA style, from his sweet little bum

of course, this is just my attempt at humor, which brings me some peace, as likewise happens when my twin brother phones me up since hearing about my upcoming open heart surgery and sings to me some of the old hymns about death that we learned when we were little boys growing up in a baptist church in the valley by the wildwoods

"life's evening sun is sinking low, a few more days and i must go" my brother croons to me as soon as i answer my phone and we both howl with laughter, knowing full well that all this is no laughing matter

but that doesn't stop him or me

he calls me late one evening and sings an old country song by wilf carter, aka montana slim, and the song is "32 wonderful years" which we as little boys used to hear our mother play on the record player and i am sure we thought it was about the end of not only his singing career, but his life

"i've no regrets, many thanks to you all, thirty two wonderful years"

we howl with laughter

my brother belts out "amazing grace" and that old funeral standby "rock of ages"

"while I draw this fleeting breath,
when mine eyes shall close in death,
when I soar to worlds unknown,
see thee on thy judgment throne,
rock of ages, cleft for me,
let me hide myself in thee."

and, i guess my point is that we all have to hide somewhere and i'm all for those who hide amidst humor and love's laughter and i can even see the sense in hiding with jesus and kale and broccoli

it beats MI and medical CVA all to hell

and it beats all to hell those who hide in violence and its serious self-righteous, godforsaken lunacy

and it beats anxiety and fear too, both of which are so serious and so heavy, when what i wish for me and for you is lightness and fun and comedy and a twinkle in the eye and a smile on our lips and laughter which is a testament to faith as much as anything

but

let me end on a serious note

on the day that doctor gary nathanson told me all about my heart he did only one thing really and he did that one thing really, really well

he took over

he said "ask me any questions you need to ask, but after this you are going to meet my assistant and she has you already scheduled today for blood work, a CT scan, and she will book you for a cardiac catheterization as soon as possible with my assistant, dr. tobin, and i have already spoken about you to dr mohan sarabu, whom we are deeply privileged to have in this area as one of the country's top heart surgeons"

none of this was on my "to do" list for that day

i had enough brain power left to ask some obvious questions that had everything to do with preparation for all this and even something to do with life's evening sun is sinking low, because i knew my brother would be singing to me soon

dr. nathanson told me that he fully expected to see me a few weeks after the surgery in his office for a follow up (that was his smart way of telling me what i wanted to hear) and then he looked me in the eyes and said "what you need to do is everything that you want to do that will make you feel ready for the surgery, so that when you lie down on the operating table you can give yourself completely into our care, having nothing on your mind because you did everything you needed and wanted to do"

on the day that doctor gary nathanson told me all about my heart he did only one thing really and he did that one thing really, really well

he took over

and he gave me peace

THE WHITE LIGHT

IN HONOR OF DR. ALANDRA TOBIN, MY CARDIAC CATHETERIZATION SPECIALIST

i think people love you more than you know, except they are flawed, self-centered, forgetful, busy, and sometimes in a bad mood

i think you love people more than it sometimes seems, except you are flawed, self-centered, forgetful, busy, and sometimes in a bad mood

everybody's got a headache at one time or another and we all get a bit short

a bit testy

even if we keep it to our very own self, which is not a bad practice, when you know it's the headache

after all, if you aren't going to announce everything about yourself to the world, why not keep your bad mood to yourself and don't take it out on others

this would contribute to world peace

this would make for adult living

i got a new grandson named victor who is nearly one year old and it is amazing that i have written so little about him, but i knew that if i started i'd never stop, so don't get me started

but i have been keeping an eye on him, and i see that, as a baby, he has no problem announcing everything to the world

everything

he has no shame

you can change his poopy diaper and he will lie there naked, look you straight in the eye, and smile as if he just painted the mona lisa

he will let you know in one second that he wants his cheerio or all his armed forces will be on full alert

tears

crying

red face

redder face

more tears

slight screaming

"i want my cheerio"

he's a very good baby, nowhere near a terrible two, and he is a very good baby because he gets lots of love and most of his cheerios

one day it will be my honor to tell him about his great grandfather

my daddy had rheumatoid arthritis for nearly forty years and hundreds gathered at his funeral because everybody there knew that if he could be so kind and thoughtful almost every moment of his life even though his fingers and toes were twisted like pretzels, then we all could be a bit better when we got a cold or had our version of a bad day, which for most of us was not pain in every joint at the level of a toothache

it's all about intention, about what the gurus call "deliberate practice"

"i will bring peace to the world, despite my pain, cause why spread the pain?"

of course a lot of the world's leaders and countries seem to have permanent migraines and they are always starting big fights as if we all have twenty lives to waste

as if life is cheap and easy to come by

the world plays ongoing russian roulette

the countries take turns, the continents take turns, the guns go off, many die, millions die

somebody's grandchild

serious, serious stuff, the stuff that does not make for peace, either inner peace or world peace it makes for lots of paperwork, posturing, motions, committees, envoys

you can't totally ignore this off the charts craziness, because it is all over the place and eventually the Bat signal is beamed up and Batman comes out of his Bat Cave and has to rescue the world with more than committees and holy intentions, and then it isn't russian roulette, then it's every chamber loaded, all bets off, people die, and then in fifty years the countries are buddies again

this, as your uncle says, is bat shit crazy

it should make for an everybody get on your knees, prostrate on your holy carpet, put on sackcloth and ashes, face mecca or jerusalem or heaven or wherever is sacred for you, weep, pray to something saner than us which we can all call Love, and confess that we are out of our ever loving minds

it is a wonder that we can have a moment's peace

this is why very smart people are often depressed or anxious, because with their finely tuned intelligence they can't totally ignore the lunacy of the world or think that a fancy new car is enough valium to take away "the world is nuts" blues

what can those of us who are not einstein do?

we can all share more cheerios

"Almost half of the world's wealth is now owned by just one percent of the population.

The wealth of the one percent richest people in the world amounts to $110 trillion. That's 65 times the total wealth of the bottom half of the world's population.

The bottom half of the world's population owns the same as the richest 85 people in the world.

In the US, the wealthiest one percent captured 95 percent of post-financial crisis growth since 2009, while the bottom 90 percent became poorer."
                                    —Oxfam International "Working for the Few"

and we need to see the light

sharing leads to more happiness than greed

every grandchild has only one life, one very precious life

precious life

the fact we forget all the time

i saw the light the other day, the white light, the kind they write about in all those end of life books

you know i always tell you the truth, including my doubts, my fears, though I do confess i'm not as good as victor, my grandson, at telling you about my poopy pants

i'm not a good painter, no mona lisa here

at any rate, the white light

the other day i was lying on an operating table receiving a cardiac catheterization where the bright doctor checks out your veins, arteries, heart and other important things with equipment that includes a knife to open your femoral artery, radioactive dye that lights up your insides, and a camera that looks for good news and bad news

they tell you that this procedure, which you pay for, has a slight chance of killing you or giving you a stroke that will make you forever forget about russian roulette

since they are not totally out of their minds, and want your money, they give you valium and benadryl by mouth before the surgery, and then valium in the bloodstream just after they put you on the operating table

now here, for peace's sake, i must detour from the white light and tell you, honey, that one day when it is either your time to go or you think it might be in the general vicinity of your time to go, all you have to do is ask for valium in the bloodstream and the angels will carry you home

you heard it here

valium in the bloodstream

even though i never knew it, i've always been the worrying sort, sort of like the rest of us

this fact has been covered over by books, a brisk keep your mouth shut old fashioned repressed scottish background, some wine, and other private tools i won't go into, except to mention that my own personal therapy radically lessened my anxiety

still, i'm the kind of guy that can write forever about peace suffice it to say, not even valium in the bloodstream can stop me from worrying that "it's my time" this time in the dim twilight of the operating room

i keep my mind off "it's my time" by looking around at all the medical stuff, at the big round x ray machine two inches from my head and heart that they whirl around as if it's a giant lego

i think of the goodness and competence of humanity that made all this possible and wish for this goodness and competence to spread to all corners of the globe, to every grandchild

wishing for peace for all, adds a bit of peace to you, even if you are somewhat awake in an operating room

i listen to the doctor say technical things back and forth to the technician who is in a booth about twenty feet to my right and back of me

this is me, elvis, finally in a recording studio, straining to hear in a sort of eavesdropping kind of way whether in their medical latin they see my death coming or a stroke storm building

"love me tender, love me true"

AND THEN THE WHITE LIGHT

but no tunnel

i asked the doctor if she saw the white light

she said "i do, what you are seeing is very bright fluorescent lights that go on when i am finished in order to make sure that i did not miss anything"

"so, it's over"

"it's over"

but, in the best sense of the word, it's not over

no, the dim twilight of fear and waiting has once again lifted and the white lights came back on and i am alive, still with a mind able to play chess, still with a heart with very clean arteries, even though no angel or valium fixed everything or found a mona lisa inside me

i wish that every leader in the world could have a cardiac catheterization i bet if they saw the white light come on there would be more world peace

precious life

the one true cheerio, victor, the one true cheerio

FIRST CLASS

IN HONOR OF TOM DIKENS, MY FRIEND

peace is made from all the little moments when people touch us with kindness, warmth, acceptance and appreciation

it is easy to not dwell on them enough, as none come with handcuffs that hold us spellbound, and so we might move on too quickly

as we look for more things

as we long for bigger things

as we await that golden moment when we know we have arrived, that we are somebody

perhaps peace is the under-rated arrival package that we can give ourselves as we remember to breathe, be grateful, see the glory in most moments, and believe (however precariously) that we are already somebody

i am finally somebody

here's how i know

tom found out that i was going to have open heart surgery, and yet i still planned to fly south and join other of his friends for a weekend celebration of his 60th birthday

he phoned and asked me if it was safe to fly, given my condition, and i told him that i have written so much about peace lately that not even cabin pressure or a shaky flight could make my heart get excited

(plus, three doctors told me "no worries" about the flight, so maybe that helped a bit too, i must admit…. man/woman does not live by his or her own word alone, but by every good word that proceedeth from the mouth of our kind experts, uplifting friends and the glorious company of blessed authors)

tom expressed his regrets about my forthcoming surgery, told me that he could not do enough about that, but said maybe it would help a bit if he upgraded me to first class for my trip to his birthday party

thank god for air miles

i am finally somebody

i flew first class

except being a creature of habit, i forgot that i was flying first class, and so i had to be reminded that it was not business as usual, economy style

"no sir, you don't have to pay for your luggage"

"sir, the first class line is over there"

"sir, breakfast is free"

"no sir, that big seat is yours alone, you don't have to share it"

the power of habit

peace is very much connected to habit

so is the nasty stuff

a couple comes for therapy and they are used to business as usual, ongoing grudge matches, persistent attack/defend loops, and the sad, sad volley of sadism and masochism as each stands their ground and gets their point across (or so they think)

peace comes when one or the other finds this extremely pointless and instead creates a series of new beginnings, a genesis of stunning, creative moments that are filled with (you guessed it) kindness, warmth, acceptance, and appreciation

"i see your point, tell me more"

"that must have hurt you, i am so sorry"

"let's stop this quarrel, and go have some fun"

"please forgive me"

"thanks for all you do for me, for all that you have done"

here is a quotation that has stuck with me for a long time, since i was 18 years old: "the mind is either a garden or a slaughter house" (hugh prather, "notes to myself") as creatures of habit, our brains can get so used to walking around in the slop of the slaughterhouse, that we can miss our garden moments or stay in the garden so briefly, even if someone or life invites us to the garden

i remember a long time ago seeing a man cry ever so gently in the first session of therapy, as he told his wife that he could not stand it when they disagreed, which had too often become their married version of a slaughterhouse

she merely carried on about one of their problems and i interrupted her quickly, and brought her back to something far more important, to the garden he had just invited her to, the garden of his heart

most of us move slowly and grudgingly from the slaughter house

something in us likes the fight, the proving of our grievances over and over again, as the fights comes with self-pity, self-righteousness, and the fact that it is all so familiar

we all are immersed in a movie of our own projections, hurts, disappointments and betrayals

this movie was created when we were very young

we did not know it was being created

the movie has a powerful script

most of the time we are certain that our movie is accurate, and that it plays in other people's brains the way we see it

and so, someone tells us with certainty their certain view that we do not like them

how easy for us to be defensive, to counter with it ain't so obvious that they like us

how hard it seems to be, to simply invite them to the garden, to let them know fully, then and there, that we love them

to display the flowers of our love

to give an overflowing river of words that speak of our gratitude, a river so clean and deep and long that it takes us miles from any view of the slaughterhouse

why not give it a try?

a long time ago a young daughter of thirty told her forty nine year old father that she had always known that her mother and he broke up because of her, because she was conceived when they were in college, and that no one in the whole family really wanted her

this view she had kept to herself until this moment in my therapy office

the father shifted his whole body towards her, put his hand on her shoulder, and said

"where did you get that view, honey? it is totally 100% mistaken wrong. on the day that your mother told me that she was pregnant, we both cried with joy. even though we were not married, we immediately threw a party for both sides of the family and i got up and announced our big news and then your mother stood up and said "if anyone in this family even mentions the word 'abortion' once to us, you will never see us again or have the privilege of seeing our longed for and already loved beautiful baby"

"as for our divorce, that had nothing to do with you, and everything to do with how young and stupid and stubborn we were about much less important things, that looked so important at the time"

the daughter cried

the father cried

i cried

TALK

IN HONOR OF DR. TOMMY TIAO FROM LUTHERAN MEDICAL CENTER, BROOKLYN, NY

the other day i felt a bit of anxiety. it wasn't the kind that would buckle your knees, as in a lion is coming after you at the zoo, when you decided to hop the fence to see if you could outrun a lion

no, this started when i was flying home from tom's birthday party and we had reached our cruising altitude of 35,000 feet

now you might guess that i was afraid of flying, and that would be a good guess, but it would be mistaken, not because it doesn't cross my mind that walking seems a far safer mode of transportation

not because it doesn't cross my mind that flying seems like an impossible dream

no, at this particular juncture in my life, worry forced its way into my brain and made me stare at some of the details involved in my upcoming open heart surgery

open heart surgery

those three words sound close to totally pleasant, almost new age-ee, what with the "open" sounding so open and "heart" sounding so heart like, but that word "surgery" suddenly throws things off in a medieval sort of direction, involving images of tables and knives and other sharp objects and a person lying on a table unable to move

and the person in this case, well that would be me, which makes it so, so different

for me

my turn

reality, not theory

stuff you can't escape with a thought, stuff that won't go away with rational, cognitive technique

the trouble with a lot of books written by rational experts of all stripes is that they are not written anywhere close to a surgical table, and so a lot of what they think works like a charm vanishes when worry is linked to very worrisome realities, like a lion running after you or when "open heart" means "let's open this guy's chest to the world" i say this not to make you worry more about the lion in your life, whatever that may be, but if we accurately assess that something is actually tougher to face than we like to imagine in our let's-pretend-fantasies, then we will actually do more to help ourselves and help one another

"this is a lion chasing you, sister, here's a gun"

"this is open you up heart surgery, brother, jesus heal you with a great big miracle or jesus come hold your hand every step of the way, especially when you can't step at all, when you are going to need something more than freud reminding you of your death wish"

amen to that

prayer sounds crazy to the current batch of rational atheists, but wild prayer is far more attuned to the desperate straits of humanity, to our desperate need for over-the-top help and ocean waves of kindness and divine levels of salvation

i am not talking about crazy prayer that is an escape from reality, where people are blamed for seeing a doctor as a lack of faith or where ongoing illness is a sign of unbelief

i am talking about sane prayer that is based on seeing how people are hurting, prayer that comes out of suffering for others, suffering for ourselves, as we moan over all the unnecessary pain, as we long for a better day for you, for me

this kind of prayer is love

jesus sweating drops of blood for himself, for you, for me

this is way more sane than irrelevant and out of touch bureaucracy, clueless business as usual politics, mere academic pontification about pain, or one sentence of advice given quickly so the giver can distance from the problem, and from the person who needs far more than our standoffish judgments about their predicament

the world seems to be run by people who are so far away from the pain

they call this "schizoid" in the therapy world, when a person goes far, far away into their head and no longer feels these matters of the heart

it is called "tin man" in the wizard of oz

the world run by tin men

by any standard, i was not feeling very tin-ee as i sat in row 20f on that airplane the other day

i began to feel squeezed

a growing pressure started to take my peace away

i felt all alone, glued not to the wonder of flying above the clouds, but glued to the upcoming fear-making surgical procedures that seem as unlikely at succeeding as thinking that a Boeing 747 can get off the ground, fly at 600 miles per hour, and land as gently as a dove on a strip of concrete

shakespeare would howl with laughter at both ideas

"you're going to fly like a bird, the whole flock of you"

"you're going to let them freeze your body to 57 degrees, basically all but stop your blood flow, and put a piece of cow in your heart"

shakespeare, in all his brilliance, would call us madder than king lear and say "you should be afraid"

despite the fact that i am a therapist, often when i have felt this kind of fear, i have kept my mouth shut and just either tried to ignore my feelings or think my way out of the (fear filled) box

the other day in row 20F i tried the talking cure

it worked

better than you can imagine

better than i ever could have imagined, despite the fact, as i say, that my profession is called the "talking cure"

i turned to the passenger next to me, whom i hadn't spoken to yet, and i looked at him and quickly assessed that he was either a high school student about 18 years old or a college student about 21 years old, heading back to new york from spring break

either that or he was from out of the country and could not speak english, which is why he had not spoken to me yet

i did not imagine that he was consumed by the "i'm not talking cause i'm all wrapped up in the keep your mouth shut silent fear of open heart surgery" cocoon "hi, my name is bob, what is your name?"

"tommy"

"are you heading back to college in new york?"

"no, I live there, but i'm on my way to another week's vacation in france and spain"

(i'm beginning to think he isn't even a college student)

"are you a college student?"

"no, i am a doctor"

"oh really, you look about 21"

"thanks, but i am actually 34 years old"

"what kind of doctor are you?"

"i am an anesthesiologist"

we had one of the loveliest talks i have ever had in my life

dear lord jesus, no wonder the lord gave us tongues to talk and ears to listen, that blessed young man took me out of myself as i asked about his life and focused away from myself and my cocoon and my fear

dear lord jesus, no wonder the lord gave us tongues to talk and ears to listen, because eventually that blessed young man explained in reassuring detail all about open heart surgery and how it made sense for the doctors to freeze the body to 57 degrees and do all the other things that seem as crazy as flying

it isn't that my own doctors have not been reassuring or explanatory, it's just that when the lion is after you, you need all the help you can get, and sometimes that help can even come from a man who looks as young as a boy, sitting next you in a metal tube going six hundred miles per hour

who knows

maybe even shakespeare was sitting in 20D and learned a thing or two

who knows

maybe the tin men will grow hearts

who knows

maybe something bigger than a lion is watching over us

who knows

maybe we are not crazy to do such crazy things as pray for one another and talk a good while and listen a lot longer

who knows

maybe we can still sing "Somewhere over the rainbow"

LOVE

IN HONOR OF MY FAMILY

samuel johnson supposedly said that "the prospect of death wonderfully concentrates the mind"

of course, since i found out on march 3rd, 2014 that i have severe aortic valve regurgitation and an ascending aortic aneurysm ("ascending" means that it is above the heart, very close to the brain artery) i have had the opportunity to test out mr. johnson's theory

just for the record, the great author's words were actually "depend upon it, sir, when a man knows he is to be hanged in a fortnight, it concentrates his mind wonderfully" and the words have a back story that are worth a minute of your google time

in the meantime, just for the record, i am not going to be hanged in a fortnight and do not think i am going to die, just yet, but lately (can you blame me?) the thought has occurred to me, the worry, the "what if?"

as far as peace goes, the prospect of death does not wonderfully concentrate the mind

it haunts the mind, splinters the mind, and ultimately distracts the mind from far lovelier things

our actual death is one big ignominious interruption, the thought of death is a million unhelpful little interruptions, sort of like the thousand nightmares you have while you are "asleep" on percoset

if you were to do a scan of my brain this past month, it would look like this: sex, fishing, open heart surgery, death; sex, fishing, open heart surgery, death; ad infinitum, with "fishing" as a stand in for every-thing else on my mind, especially the glory of working and the glory of love

(daddy freud was right: "love and work are the cornerstones of our humanness")

now some would say that i am focusing on the negative, but that's not how this stuff works

it works just like all the other shitty stuff of life, pardon my french

the very bad stuff grabs you from the great swamp and hauls you under and it forces you to dwell in darkness, it takes root in you, it swims in you, it all but fills you

it's the same for all of us

the man whom you thought would love you forever leaves you in a heartbeat, with no warning, and all you think about, all you feel, first thing in the morning, and every third thought is "my life is over"

you are a cute teenager, or so they say, but one morning you wake up with either one huge pimple or a face full of acne and, as far as you are fully concerned, you may as well join the circus because all that the kids in town are going to smirk about is your hideous face

you're not focusing on it, it is the only thing in sight, a pimple as big as mount everest for all the world to see

it's the same for all of us

you have no money. you lost your job. you are 55. you are not focusing on fear. you are scared out of your ever loving mind. fear consumes you. peace has left town

the fear of death is no different

ask not for whom the bell tolls, and it tolls loudly or (what's worse) very quietly and perniciously, deep in our soul, no wonder some drink

the "answer" to all this muck is basically the same, though i do not like the word "answer," because that doesn't quite convey how miserable and powerful the muck is, and how hard it is at times to get out of the dark filled swamp

the answer, plain and simple is to live, to live large, to take yourself seriously, to stop wasting your f'ing time (as i literally, with much love, told one of my seminar attendees this past while), to know in the depths of your being that everything about you (well, almost everything) is unique and marvelous, even your face with the pimple that is smaller than you think, and the great, great thing is that despite death down the road we still have one another and we still have possibility (way more fish in the sea) and we can endure and get to better days and we can haul one another up from the swamp of darkness to the light of dry land and blue skies and better days, and it is this latter venture, the venture of love, that will give you peace more than anything

this happened to me this week

i was doing therapy with a couple of beautiful souls and the man happens to have a beautiful baritone voice, and he almost made it to the Metropolitan opera, and i think would have, if his parents had bothered to give him one compliment in the first twenty years of his life

(listen up. silence is not golden. the coney island voices of craziness play in our brain constantly, so even the playing field and give yourself and others lots of real, authentic, honest, genuine compliments. it can't hurt. silence won't get you on stage at the met or anywhere. give voice to the good things. let your light shine, others need it, you need it, it is an order from jesus

a lot of clients have told me this week that i have to make it through surgery because it took them years to find a therapist who would actually talk to them, give them lots of ideas and options, and do more than just ask "how does that make you feel?" this is true, so i ain't bragging, and besides, ralphie baby, my much loved therapist, taught me how to be this way, since he spoke to me often in riveting tones, to bring me back from the swamp, and one of those times once included the words "i don't give a f. how you feel, or that your feelings are hurt by me, it is time for you to grow up"

and all this from an episcopal priest)

anyway, back to the couple

i got the bright idea during the session to ask the man if he could sing "nessun dorma" and he said he didn't know the piece, so i took out my iPad and in a minute had pavarotti singing to us

oh how lovely

glorious fishing

of course the man actually knew the piece, just had forgotten the name, but said it wasn't meant to be sung by a baritone

and then i got a brighter idea

over thirty years ago, music/movie/book genius friend carl played "The Pearl Fishers Duet" by bizet for me, sung by jussi bjoerling and robert merrill

i am not a classical music buff by any means, but i have never forgotten it, though i have not heard it in years

i asked the couple if they knew the piece, and they didn't

so i found it on my iPad and played it for them

do you remember the moment in "shawshank redemption" when andy dufresne breaks into the superintendent's office and plays "Canzonetta sull'aria" from Mozart's "Marriage of Figaro" over the loudspeakers so that throughout the whole prison all the inmates hear the music and they stop their fighting and their working and their grumbling and they just look up at the sky enraptured and enfolded in grace this happened to me with the "Pearl Fishers Duet" and this couple

the woman, a talented and sensitive artist, got tears in her eyes

the man got tears in his eyes

i got tears in my eyes

no one spoke

the music took over

death was gone, everything bad was gone, and for a moment we saw that everything good is lovely beyond our imagination, beyond our telling

everything good is what brings us peace

everything good

it hauls us up from the swamp

two stories: the first being a story that i have never told anyone, the second a story of what i did today, the day before my open heart surgery

a long time ago when i was 21 years old i lived in a swamp of darkness, loneliness, fear and almost 100% hopelessness when it came to certain things like getting married or having solid confidence or making much of a difference to anyone

a lot of this was a good case of self-pity as i later found out in therapy when ralphy baby screamed at me and told me that self-pity was my poison, even though he knew and empathized with everything bad that had dragged me into the swamp, amazed as he was that it did not send me into the back wards of a mental asylum

nevertheless, i wasn't feeling too good back then, and what i have never told anyone is that i wanted to die

i remember walking late at night down by the pond at my college feeling so alone, and lonely, so over-whelmed, so not peaceful, shall we say it's not that i had a death wish. colleague arlin assures me that daddy freud was wrong about the whole death wish idea, and should be shot for it, given the misery and blame that theory has spread. we don't have a death wish. we just have a i am sick and tired of the swamp wish

listen

what kept me alive was you, it's always been you

you my dear twin brother (who, by the way, knowing laughter is a way out of the swamp, knowing laughter is a defense mechanism, phoned me this week and kept up the recent tradition of songs, asking three of his Tyndale Seminary colleagues to join him in a quartet as they sang "in the sweet bye and bye, we shall meet on that beautiful shore"   ....i howled with laughter)

what kept me alive was you

you, all my smart friends, whom i am thinking of now by name, each of you

you, my most courageous daddy, living, i believe, rheumatoid arthritis free, in the sweet bye and bye

you, my mommy, who taught me without words the depth of human pain and coaxed empathy from my soul, as a little boy

you, all my good relatives in canada and scotland and australia and the united states, whom i am thinking of now by name, each of you

you, my unexpected wife and adorable kids and new adorable grandson, baby victor

you, my parishioners, who taught me the ropes, when i was so young

you, my doctors and nurses, who have so often offered me your hard won competence

you, my clients, you have trusted me with your swamps, and hungered for my words

you, my teachers and ministers and therapists and colleagues, you have given voice to my gifts, and your words have saved me

you, my readers, and a few of you in particular, and you know who you are, you have believed in my voice as a writer and your affirmation has made all the difference in the world, along with my brother who told me one night in the middle of the night that if i didn't start writing more he would come down to pough-keepsie, ny and shove a pencil up my ass to get me moving and this from a theologian of note

what kept me alive was you, it's always been you

there is no peace without the other, without community, without you

on the day before my open heart surgery, i will be preaching at the church i attend as my dear minister, bob geehan, is off to dallas, texas to meet his first grandchild, a little baby named emma

i figure it's not a bad idea to preach the day before open heart surgery, sort of putting in a good example of myself to the heavens, if you know what I mean

i will be preaching a sermon called "The Gospel in Two Words." it's based on the story of a blind man begging jesus to heal him as jesus passes by with his entourage of disciples and the throng of important people who want to be near the miracle man. saint mark tells us that the man shouted for jesus to heal him and the crowd told the man to be quiet

and then these two beautiful words

"jesus stopped"

"jesus stopped and said 'call him.'"

what kept me alive was you, it's always been you

i will lay down on the operating table tomorrow, so grateful, so grateful for each of you who have stopped for me

and i will lie there knowing to my core that any human being who stops in love for another human being is jesus, and is on the side of jesus, whether they know it or not

what kept me alive was you, it's always been you

TRUST

IN HONOR OF DR. MOHAN SARABU, MY HEART SURGEON

oh my god

words cannot describe what it is like waking up 18 hours or more after your head hit the pillow on an operating table where you are to undergo a surgery that is routine, to everyone in the room but you

it seems like an eternal two seconds have passed, and you "come to" and realize that you are alive, alive to another day that is unfathomably better than anything you could win at a lottery store

words cannot describe what it is like to wait in the holding room with your family before such a serious surgery, when everyone whispers or chokes up in your ear about loving you, and whispers that everything will be ok, when in the back of everyone's mind, or at least mine, there is the thought, the not very peaceful thought, that this could be the final goodbye

nevertheless, they come and get you and wheel you away

i comforted myself with anything i could get my hands on and when one nurse named lynda came up and told me that my wife taught all her children in grade one and that "we'll take care of you," well, I could have burst into tears right there in that most sterile environment, where every drop of liquid has to accounted for, where everything is done with precision, where messy things like human moods do not run the show

nevertheless, i clung to those five words with all my heart

"we'll take care of you"

i comforted myself with anything i could get my hands on and when tyson, the man who runs the bypass machine, came over to introduce himself because he was a next door neighbor to one of my clients, and had been expecting me that morning, it helped me imagine that this was a place where everybody knew my name

i comforted myself with the fact that we all are truly in one another's hands, and there comes a time when we must trust in others, those who are worthy of it

most of all, i trusted my surgeon with complete faith, because all you have to do is mention his name in the hudson valley in matters of medicine and the human heart, and all you hear is awe, gratitude, respect and trust and that is largely what you do through the whole healing process

you trust in others

the healing process, like the path to peace itself, consists of step by step largely grunt work, that is very clearly set forth by experts, experts of the body, experts of the soul

you cough holding a pillow to your chest, you breathe into that spirally thing, you walk when they tell you to, you don't push up with your arms, ad glorious infinitum

i had a secret weapon too

i had a picture of my grandson smiling away at his first birthday, cake all over his mouth, holding up his left forefinger so that the whole world would know how old victor is

i never took his picture out of my sight, and i made a vow to him. i told him that i would not complain about anything and that i would do everything they told me, because i wanted to make many more of his birthdays and play golf with him and uncle aaron, my son, and play many games with my wife, cindy, who is his grammy , his mother michelle, my daughter, and auntie laura, my first born

i told him that i would be supremely grateful to everyone who helped me, from the people who cleaned my room to the patient care technicians who cleaned me up every day, until i could finally head to the shower room, appropriately situated next to a door called "Dept. of Environmental Services"

when they pulled tubes out of me, on various days, i would look away from the procedure, and focus on his smiling face

and when i felt pain, i took the pain in and received it, asking the universe in a mystical way to cancel some future pain of his and transfer it to me

do not mistake me, this was all assisted by whatever peace team concocted those narcotics

do not mistake me, i am not some superhero who can stand lots of pain

but i am good at grunt work, at enduring through emotional pain and physical pain, waiting for the better day to come, step by step making it come, imperfectly, slowly, but most of the time heading in the right direction

what more can we ask?

do not mistake me. this was no joy ride or some sentimental journey. once dr. nathanson diagnosed me, about a month before my surgery, i attempted to get all my affairs in order, just in case

i tell you this only because it takes far longer to get things in order than you can imagine, especially if you are a failed obsessive, as most of us are

the quantity of peace in someone's life is directly related to having things in order, because we are more overwhelmed when things are in disarray

peace comes in accepting the mess that is inevitable, peace comes in fighting against the mess that need not be

and so, inevitably, in this case, a few messes did show up, most with the name of atrial fibrillation where your heart goes out of its normal sinus rhythm, into one that the doctors do not like

this is a somewhat common side effect of open heart surgery, and it made me miss an early trip home by a couple of days, but to tell you the truth i was glad for the extra time to recover in the cardiac step down unit (time made all the more acceptable by the fact that i was being helped by people from all over the world, experts at every turn, and, for me, without exception, experts at kindness and warmth)

my afib did not go away as soon as they wanted, and so they started to gather the team that would shock my heart with paddles and jolt it back into sinus rhythm

(my mother-in-law, a lovely woman from the spanking generation, thought this meant they were going to paddle me on my behind, to which all my scottish relatives will laugh at our inside joke as we sing "put ice cream on my bum and spank me, i love it")

one of the things that i "wanted" to do before going into the hospital was to make a final secret goodbye video for my family and friends.

just in case

 i never got around to it, but as my heart kept carrying on and making a fuss, before the paddle squad came, i took out my Ipad and made my own little spielberg movie, tears and all

alone in the room, i sobbed

this certainly doesn't sound like positive thinking, but i believe that genuine peace can only come when we face things, when we name what life is like, and head straight into the waves again, do not mistake me. i am not a professional at facing everything, full steam ahead. i know how to avoid, deny, delay, and put a spin on things that is not 100% accurate. we do need our defenses: "mankind cannot bear very much reality" (t.s. eliot)

peace is the complex land between fantasy and reality, and peace is composed of both

a half an hour later after my movie making career had started, the nurse came into my room with a smile on her face and said "your sinus rhythm is back, and i order you to keep it that way"

maybe i jolted myself back into sinus, or maybe it was the unpronounceable drug they gave me

and so, a day later, i was chauffeured home by my wife, five days before easter, with me in the back seat, protected against a steering wheel and air bags, in case of an accident

please do not tell dr. sarabu, but i was high as we drove home

high on life

intoxicated with gratitude, for all those who have loved me, especially my family

so buzzed to see the green grass, the tulips by my mailbox, even a cloudy sky

the mature, the seasoned, the wise, the alive, shall stare at life, at babies, at rivers, at a sunrise now and then, at a starry, starry night, at a beautiful body, at every blessed thing that does no harm, at every blessed person that brings no harm, at every blessed person that shines their holy light

this all, all of this and more, is what brings us peace, if we are wise enough to receive it

THE END?

and so, what if the catastrophic had happened, which dr. sarabu mentioned as a possibility, and this all had not ended well, for the time being?

well, then, i would not have been able to write these last few sections, or tell you that, despite pain and tubes down the throat, life is unbearably lovely and worthy of gratitude and e.e. cummings praise

i would not have been able to tell you that there are no words for having your wife and children whisper in your left ear in the cardiac critical care unit what they whispered over 24 hours before in the waiting room outside the operating room before you left everything behind and put your trust in very calm and competent people

they whispered, "i love you"

i would not have been able to tell you that when they take the tubes out of your throat and give you ice chips to swallow and eventually a small sip from a glass of water, that this is the best drink in the world

instead, i am alive and i get to tell you that what follows is all cliché and yet the clichés are completely and profoundly true

love yourself

love others

follow your dreams

step on the gas

slow down

enjoy the journey

ask for more help

get some of that help from experts

give more help

admit your brokenness

PEACE ETC.

fix some things about yourself

have more fun

watch more comedies

live better

understand that life is an amazing miracle and gift

there is no time to waste

and, this i promise: you will have more peace

when i woke up from over 18 hours of unconsciousness, my first thought was "i am alive" and i was calmly glad

it's hard to be anything more than calm, when you are so sedated, and i basically think they have you tied to the bed, so you cannot get up and dance

a while later, still in the middle of the night, i suddenly remembered that i had forgotten to tell a relative or a colleague to leave a message on my main psychotherapy answering machine about my (hopefully) successful surgery

i had promised this to my clients, whom i love

this gave me a bit of a panic, because i knew that certain clients would have me dead and gone from this world if there was no new message on my machine

you should try communicating this to your private nurse as you are coming out of anesthesia, unable to speak, hands all puffy and filled with tubes, in the dim light of a quiet intensive care unit

i managed with hand gestures to get her to understand that some sort of phone call needed to be made, but by then she noticed my blood pressure was rising and she kindly but firmly ordered me to stop and rest quietly and told me that it would have to wait until the morning

blood pressure rising just after open heart surgery did not sound too appealing, even to my non-medical mind, and so i gave up something i could not control and did what i often advise my clients to do

i rested my heart on its good intentions, forgave myself, and went back to a peaceful sleep we are all failed obsessives, imperfect perfectionists, built for heaven, bound to earth

still, what if all had not gone well, is there any hope for peace then?

to respond to this is about as easy as trying to communicate a message when all parties concerned are recovering from anesthesia and unable to speak, with hearts ripped apart by emotional pain, by doubt, by evil and suffering, by bad religious experiences, or none at all

but i will try

there is no answer for the unspeakable tragedies, natural and man-made, that are part of our daily existence

"do no harm" is the well advised medical oath that applies to each of us, who have one another's lives in our hands, just as much, though not as obviously, as dr. sarabu and his team had my life
in their hands

if we live better, there will be less tragedy, more peace

this is all cliché and yet the clichés are completely and profoundly true

to those who have suffered great loss, like the loss of a child, this is a pain that will never go away, but with lots of help that pain can lessen

as for your death, here is what i know and what i wish for you

about 16 years ago i actually had my first open heart surgery for a leaky aorta valve, and despite the fact there was no aortic aneurism, the recovery did not go as smoothly

for some reason, my stomach stopped working and i gained 18 lbs. of fluid in one day and was closer to congestive heart failure and the pearly gates

in terms of energy, i had never felt so empty and for the first time could taste the fact that, if we are lucky, one day we will welcome death with open arms and know that it is time

time also for valium in the bloodstream or morphine

still, what about the pearly gates?

again, metaphorically, with a tube down my throat and tubes in my puffy hands, with barely the ability to tap this kind of message, can i say for now that all i ask is that you consider the possibility of heaven, not for me, maybe not even for you, but only for all those who never had a chance for peace, whose lives were broken at the start by where they were born or what was done to them, eternal life for those born with terrible diseases, with no shot at life at all, eternal peace for those crushed by all the crazy dictators who themselves must not have a moments peace, or if they do, they are out of their minds

the wish for heaven is a wish for justice, a wish for a second chance for those who had none at all, even more it is a wish for peace for this whole crazy, broken, wonderful world

this is my wishful thinking

in a world where people wish for far worse, in a world where pain is so real, can you blame me for such a wish?

INTERVIEW

IS THERE ANYTHING YOU WOULD LIKE TO EMPHASIZE AGAIN OR SAY FOR THE FIRST TIME ABOUT THIS WHOLE ADVENTURE YOU HAVE EXPERIENCED?

I cannot stress enough how long it takes to get your things in order. Most of us, while preparing for major surgery, if we are lucky enough to have time to prepare, already have a full life, so it's not like we can assign everything to our valet and work 24/7 on wills, health proxies, banking details and the like. Nor is it easy to do all this when you have something looming on your mind that seems way more important than any detail you have to attend to.

ANYTHING ELSE IN TERMS OF PREPARATION?

Before you go into surgery, you should get everyone who is there with you to go over "Is there anything I have forgotten?"

Family members will never regret telling you in words and hugs their deepest love. And the family should be ready for the fact that once the operating team reps come to get you, they have their own agenda and "it is time" means they want the show to hit the road. Be prepared that this moment of separation will suddenly happen and may be the hardest that either patient or family will endure. Hopefully.

WHAT ABOUT THE ACTUAL PAIN OF RECOVERY FOR A MAJOR SURGERY LIKE YOU HAD?

Of course, all surgeries are different, and pain thresholds are different. In my experience, the best thing to do is to take it a step at a time and do everything they tell you to do. Step by step makes all the difference in the world. Don't trust that your feelings are an accurate measure of how you are doing. For example, the day after surgery I would have taken a vow never to have this surgery again, because, as they say, you feel like you have been hit by a truck, even though the drugs work wonders. By the end of my hospital stay, I was already saying "I will do this again, if I have to."

Through the whole healing process, you feel present and clear-headed, but when you look back it seems like you were in much more of a fog than you realized. It takes time for your head to clear, so make sure you have someone checking your decisions, medicine and important daily details.

Also, it is quite likely that you will have less patience and tolerance during recovery. After all, your body has been dealt a major blow, your energy is at an all-time low, and everything you do will feel like work. Plus, no matter how accepting you or I might be when something like this happens, no matter how grateful we are to be alive, there must be a part of us that is really angry at this turn of events. In the fifth week of my recovery, I could sense that my brain was starting to slip into the defense mechanism called "splitting" where we make people either all bad or all good. I have trained myself to basically keep my mouth shut when I am in this state, because it is very primitive—and following the lead of one's darkness can turn friends into enemies and cause needless, exaggerated pain.

HOW WAS YOUR ANXIETY THROUGH THIS WHOLE PROCESS? DID YOU LEARN ANYTHING NEW ABOUT FEAR?

I had way less fear this go round than my first open heart surgery in 1998. This time I was much closer to home and had more family present, more visitors in general. And before my surgery I received word from so many people around the world who were pulling for me that I sort of floated on a cloud of love. I think my friend, Paul Upham, had every Catholic in the world saying a prayer for me. And so, I learned through experience, that love is more powerful than fear and makes all the difference in the world. This isn't to say that every moment was peachy, but that other people make a bigger difference than they can possibly imagine to the sick person who is feeling so vulnerable, possibly so alone, so small in the big scheme of things. Likewise, even though the doctors and nurses and patient care technicians have so much to do, I think it would be hard for them to fathom how someone in my shoes (or, I guess not in any shoes) clings to their every word, every look, as sign that things are ok and that you matter to them.

But...

BUT?

You do matter to them. Initially, you feel and hope that you are the center of their world, that they are doing everything in their power to get you back to blessed, blessed health, or as much semblance of that as you are capable of. But eventually you realize, as a minor narcissistic normal blow, that they have their lives to attend to, their worries, their bills, and, hopefully, their loved ones. And the next round of patients will follow you and pretty soon you will take a back seat in importance, not because you were actually unimportant, but because going to the hospital is like most things in life—we meet strangers, fellow students, colleagues and neighbors in mainly a moment by moment fashion and then we go our separate ways. Hopefully, in that moment or series of moments, we do no harm and add some good to one another's lives.

The upshot of this is that we all should value the steady people in our lives way more than we often do. It is wonderful that Dr. Sarabu saved my life, and I will never forget him, but it is the steady people in my life (family, friends, colleagues, clients) who truly make it worth living.

THE BIGGEST LESSONS IN ALL THIS?

Don't do life alone, don't do anything like surgery alone. If you have no friends or family, start reaching out to people in kindness, pay attention to them, and your world will expand in a very necessary way. There is no time to waste. The details of what matters and what doesn't is a very complex topic, but facing what I did makes one realize on the one hand that everything matters and, on the other hand, it is so easy to do stuff and own stuff and think stuff that doesn't amount to a hill of beans.

Life is so precious.

Of course, "everything fades" as Irwin Yalom says, so it is hard to remember and live these truths or almost anything else I wrote about in this book. This is another reminder why we need one another: to keep one another awake, to be there for one another, in joy and in sorrow, to keep our perspective. When I was in the hospital, one nurse asked a patient care technician to walk thirty feet and get something for her. The tech complained a bit and I said to her, "No offense, but I would gladly trade places with you." We all laughed.

THEORY AND ACTION

THE THOUSAND LITTLE THINGS

peace comes in little pills, like klonopin, and it comes in little moments like when the hug really got through to you because she held on for a little bit longer and hugged your back a little bit tighter and it dawned on even you that she wanted to kiss you and even though you never kissed, the very thought of it kicked your self-doubt to the curb for at least one solid day and your so-called dirty mind went to town with that almost kiss on many a night, making it bigger than it was, adding to it with a little bit of imagination that came easily in those days, attached as it was to the fire of youth and the fire of life

and, for peace sake, for god's sake, for your sake, though it would take years to think it through, it dawned on you that what is really dirty is football for what it does to men's knees and backs and brains, war is filthy and that needs no explanation, neglect is dry caked dirty mud, people not bothering with you and you not bothering with them is the lazy dirt and shame of us, but kissing and hugging and hot baths and massages and little pills that ease the pain or little pills that make things work and hands touching you in soft and hopefully hard places, this is not dirty, this is love delivered in such a visible form that is often the truest communion, followed as it often is by blessed sleep, far better than a cigarette

love delivered in such a visible form is what we often need in order for peace to find us, because we have gotten so used to love's obvious forms like meals made, money made, dishes done, clothes cleaned and folded and put away, that it often takes us to be alone and calming down in a motel room before we count our blessings, before we taste anew the thousand little things that are part of our kingdom, the thousand little things that give us peace, if only we knew it, before it is too late, before we blow everything up in our entitlement, bouts of anger, the slow, insidious taking everything for granted, and self-righteous certitude that we could easily, easily do better

and sometimes we can do better, and must do better, that is for sure, when all we have is mess and no wish on both parties part to fix it

peace to those who have the courage to go for better, when hell surrounds you

peace to those who struggle with such a tough decision

peace to those who know there is no place like home, wherever home may be

peace comes in little thoughts that oh so easily sound like clichés, but listen to them anyway, dwell on them anyway, dwell in them anyway

"easy does it"

"a day at a time"

"the peace of the lord be with you"

"walk in the light"

"love casts out fear"

"all things shall be well"

"don't borrow trouble"

"i love you"

"let the day's own trouble be sufficient for the day"

"we love you"

"breathe"

"live in the present"

these sayings by jesus, by bill w. and his friends, by therapists, by your friends, by julian of norwich, these little words are not clichés to those who spoke them or wrote them or bothered to pass them on. these little words are communion bread, sacramental wafers, and wine turned into blood, delivered through waves of anxiety, through grey doubt, around episodes of harmful drinking, amidst wild storms of insignificance, against all odds, against opposition within and without, often at the cost of actual blood shed

an attractive woman puts on her lipstick, and you think it is so that she will look even better, but what you don't know is that she thinks she is ugly and the lipstick takes away a bit of the doubt as she heads off to church where she will say "the peace of the lord be with you" because in that moment she wants you to see her, to notice her significance, and she hopes that you know this little moment is only the be-ginning, not the end, and what she craves, what we all crave, is more words than that, more touch than that, but this is a good start and way better than nothing, nothing being the dirty thing we often do

or maybe she heads off to AA and she says that she is an alcoholic and she is welcomed with a hello, and she feels safe in the company of the anxious, the desperate, the lonely, who willingly confess their need for the clichés because the clichés work better than too much of what has not worked, but here too she wants more, like we all do, she wants someone to take her home, to love her as if that were the major point of their existence, and she wants to love someone else in that way too, as if it were the major part of her existence, but she will be content to go home with the holy wish that she will love herself more in the meantime

and when we say to her "take care" and "take good care of yourself" this is not a brush off, because our home is already full and we can't take her home, and yet in that moment those little words are well and truly meant and we hope she will take them to heart. and she tells us to "take good care" and she means it too because she can see our lovely hands, our beautiful eyes, our hard won effort to grab on to some peace and to pass it on

the passing of the peace, surely the point of all music and art and poetry, the point of all faith, the point of words and pills, the point of sex, the point of home

my oldest daughter took my youngest daughter to see elton john the other night for her thirtieth birthday present and when i heard that that talented, talented man sang his heart out for two and a half hours, singing all his glorious hits, one after another, i got all choked up because i knew that in some unfathomable way he had brought peace to my little girls and all who were in the audience, and there is something in me that wants to shout that he, sir elton, is a priest, a gospel singer, a minister, as much as billy graham, at least in all those glorious moments as music filled the air, as the air was not filled with gun shots, bombs, cruel words, all the dirty things

all the dirty things seem so big and powerful. we can't help but notice them, in fact are somehow sickeningly drawn to them in order to prove that we are big boys and big girls who can handle talk of foul play, the coming apocalypse, despair, and the death of everything. but we are not big enough boys and girls to handle such dread, even though we may think otherwise. we can't stare at the sun and we can't stare at death. we have to look away, otherwise we will go blind and become as numb as the newscasters flipping through pages of disaster with smiles on their faces, hoping their ratings will go up

staring at disaster. oh how foolish. for immature audiences only

the mature, the seasoned, the wise, the alive, shall stare at life, at babies, at rivers, at a sunrise now and then, at a starry, starry night, at a beautiful body, at every blessed thing that does no harm, at every blessed person that brings no harm, at every blessed person that shines their holy light

the mature, the seasoned, the wise, the alive, shall read gospel truth, the little words of guidance and warmth and love that come in expected (read clichés) and unexpected ways

i have a relative who, some years back, made good acquaintance with klonopin, when he was up to his eyeballs in a unique sort of anxiety that we called "bonkies." at this period in my life, i was friends with a famous person, who happened to be a christian, and he was thinking of taking klonopin for his version of anxiety and he wanted to know what i thought about it. i told him that i thought we all needed all the help we could get and that the drug worked wonders for many of my clients and my relative. i told him that my relative took the pill and that he was so grateful for it that just before he took it he said "the body of christ given for me." this made my friend roar with laughter and eased his mind to order up a batch for himself

he talks about it to this day

you might try more talking, we need all the help we can get

the body of christ

you might try some clichés

the body of christ

you might try more kisses

the body of christ

and you might understand that you are the body of christ for someone. you are their peace, their soothing, their love

WE NEED SOUP

we were all sad around these parts because a train went off the tracks going fast around a bend that is every inch a bend and something had to give and what gave was four lives lost and dozens injured and when it's this close to home it is not a statistic or a story it is pain and horror and weeping and fear

one of my clients was in the first car and she could feel that the train was going too fast but she is smart and into accuracy and she wouldn't swear to this (to a detective) because she doesn't ride the train very much but she nevertheless would swear that she knew something was going very wrong and all of a sudden she was thrown around the train like a balloon being blown by the wind and she did not end up where she thought she was going to end up safely at grand central meeting a friend for some continuing ed and some continuing fun

instead she ended up almost in the hudson river, inside a train car that had flipped 360, and when the spin was over she took stock of herself and realized that she wasn't badly hurt, and after she did what she could for those who were worse off, she went back to her broken seat, put on her coat with a hood on it and she pulled the hood way over her head and face and she closed her eyes and she snuggled into that seat and she said a prayer for herself and for everybody else on that godforsaken train and she sat there and waited for help

sometimes the only thing to do is close our eyes so we do not look at what we should never have to look at

sometimes we need to pull the wool over our eyes

sometimes things are that godforsaken

sometimes all we can do is wait

and we wait mostly for friends and colleagues and loved ones but sometimes the loved one is the stranger whose blessed hands pull us away, pull us out, touch us, hold us, guide us, blanket us, and bring us to safety, safety being the ordinary space that will now forever look miraculous because we have lost our innocence

and how can those who have lost their innocence ever have peace again?

and what about those who never had innocence in the first place, will you close your eyes and say a prayer for them?

and how can anyone believe in god in such a godforsaken world?

and, so, we wait around and hang out around these questions, we scared, hurt, broken people who wonder sometimes if anyone really cares for us, or cares for very long

and we scared, hurt, broken people also secretly wonder if anyone really knows us, feels like us, understands how scared and broken we are, how lonely we feel as we desperately try mainly to show the other side of us, the competent side, the side that pretends we can handle anything and we don't really need one another

and then something like a train wreck happens and we know in our bones that we need one another, depend on one another, love one another and we see that we are all in this together, and for a while this is a truth that we will live by, until things get back to normal and we go back to our normal reserve, our normal defensiveness against our raw baby like dependency on one another

and in our dependency we are not very much soothed by thought and logic and proof and wordy answers

we want those blessed hands, we want home, we want our blankets, we want hugs and kisses, we want water and warmth, we want our mommy and our daddy, we want soup

and for now, this is heaven enough, it is the beginning of peace, the ordinary that is miracle, the human touch that is divine

VIOLENT ALTERATIONS

this is being written twelve days before christmas but it almost doesn't matter if it was written twelve days before any day because it is always quite likely that you are in a rush and the man with a gun is chasing you which is most undeserved and most unfortunate because you already have too much to do unless you have nothing to do which is the worst and so either way you need and want a lot more peace but, frankly, there isn't a whole lot of time to get it or there is too much time to get it and that huge empty space will have you reeling with too many options and not enough necessity

"whenever a person is faced in life with a choice, his whole being trembles with the dilemma of what to do. It trembles because, being human he wants both things but can't have both; because deciding always means being altered; and because alteration, however desirable, is always violent. Anxiety is the stage a person has to pass through on his way to creating himself" (daniel smith "monkey mind: a memoir of anxiety")

and so, some violent alterations for you, offered in a hurry because i have to take out the garbage, vacuum the stairs, straighten some books, go pick up a prescription for cialis which is not true but i thought the laugh would give you a moment's peace and will have my brother in canada in stitches and meanwhile say i was to go get cialis who can afford the four hours not to mention the terror which would accompany the four hours are these people serious?

where were we? oh yes, violent alterations...here are some:

breathe

pause often to be grateful

walk

state very specifically exactly how you are guilty, if you are guilty, and do something about it like stop doing the thing that makes you feel guilty, or do the thing you should do, or apologize and say you are sorry

these blessed violent alterations stop the rush and the man with the gun backs off

decide to be a unique person with personal ceo power over your life, so when you are spinning like a top with too many options it is far better to order yourself to pick one thing and go do it rather than sit in the shit of anxiety which is where the devil will easily get you and twist your insides for an hour and all you'll have to show for it is an hour sitting in a chair feeling like the s word and looking pale

sorry, about the s word, can't think of a better word to describe anxiety

more violent alterations:

don't yell from one floor to another floor to another person in your house, even from one room to another, since you have to raise your voice and people will interpret this as anger or rebuke or criticism and besides it is far better to go for a tiny walk to be in front of them and hug them and in a soft voice say "where did you put the whatchamacallit?"

and you burn calories

do not assume that you are the cause of all evil, including the cause of all your anxiety, unless you went out and drugged your brain into oblivion or are burglarizing homes every night; other than that, anxiety is the human condition and there is lots to be scared about that you did not create as in very long snakes, planes that go 600 miles per hour, cars that go 88 feet per second, and things that go bump in the night

i say this because i hear all the time that people are told that they are making themselves crazy and i wonder if they go into the basement and get out some hammers and nails and make their actual monkey mind or brain that is so susceptible to finding fear and dwelling on it

which is not how it works because nobody dwells on fear, that would be really crazy

the truth is far more cruel

fear dwells on us

it has a life of its own and it pounds on us, beats us into submission and sometime we do not like this one bit, it makes us cry and tremble and crawl into a fetal position and if we have that kind of fear it is usually because people have been very, very mean to us and those people are usually the ones who were supposed to be very, very kind to us, like our uncle or father or sister

it's not that i'm not into occasional, on target blame, it's just that i find blame very over used, very over-rated and often very poorly used especially upon kind, gentle souls who deserve a break from incessant blame

so declare your innocence, your good intentions, the good work you do

do not borrow trouble is one of the great violent alterations that i say often to myself and to other people and i do not say it with glib superiority or a sense that it will easily get somebody out of a fetal position like offering candy to a baby but it is worth the try because it is the godawfulest most truest statement in the world when it comes to anxiety

because for each of us what we actually should worry about will become glaringly obvious as in your teenager is out of their mind or you have to pay your taxes or the red light is coming on in your car or the mole on your neck is looking dark

speaking about a mole on your neck i had one a couple of years ago and my bright doctor andrew chernack told me to have it looked at by a dermatologist and i asked him if i should worry about it and he said a violent thing to me, he said "no, don't worry about it, do something about it"

and that's all we can do, isn't it? all along the way, do something about it

doing

the violent alternative to worry

CRYING

i wish you peace because i am afraid that you are afraid of the night, that you are afraid in the night and i wish you peace because i fear that that you are aware of how precarious everything good is in this world, how dark and powerful the dark is, and i wish you peace because though you might feel amused and proud that you have personally done as well as you have, you might also be noticing more vividly and painfully all the ways in which you have not done well, and you probably think you do not make that much of a difference

you make more difference than you think, trust me

and yet you do not need to be told how insignificant, ineffective, small, unimportant, and unnoticed we all can feel, from time to time, especially when we listen to the howling winds and hawkers of apocalypse and death who jack up the ratings for their tv channel and basically nasty brand of faith

i wish you peace because you might feel like a nobody

and yet, still, holy blessed still, you yearn to know that you are somebody, because deep down you have at least a glimmer that you are already somebody

i wish you peace because i know just a touch of how awful it is to not feel peace and self-worth and i think of many people i have listened to who are ravaged and rearranged by such unutterable agony that it is a wonder that therapy schools and ministry schools and political schools and teacher schools and journalism schools and writing schools and lawyer schools and doctor schools and nurse schools and any schools that exist to help people aren't schools, first and mainly, for nothing but crying

crying should be the major curriculum for anybody who has anything to do with people

the hawkers of apocalypse and death rarely cry

i am ashamed to tell you once again that since the last time i told you about this very thing i have heard many a christian chatter away about the eternal damnation of a human being they knew and still to this day, with sixty years of living under my belt, i have not ever seen one of them even get choked up about this kind of pronouncement

how about those of us who call ourselves christians buy a full page ad in the new york times and apologize to the world for our heartless insensitivity?

imagine if every therapist and holy person and politician and reporter and writer and lawyer and doctor and nurse could not graduate until he or she could cry as freely as a baby, cry naturally every day at the mere mention of human pain; imagine if all these people could not matriculate until they knew how to work with lifelong utter devotion towards the alleviation of pain, mainly through empathy and understanding and action, and not one bit through empty promises and aloof diagnosis and heartless laws and a million words that make no difference

and can we say as loudly as ever before that all the leaders whose curriculum is violence and oppression, they are the insignificant ones, the ones whose worth should be questioned, the ones who are unimportant, the ones who are so far off the mark, those poisoned by and poisoning us with their curriculum of cold indifference and frozen hatred and endless rounds of revenge covered over by their stage show of false caring before they hop into their limo and head back to cold, empty palaces

the dark is dark and powerful, but what you need to know and feel and dance to and dwell on with all your blessed wishing-for-peace heart is that the darkness has not overcome the light, and there are still so many somebodies waiting to be loved, so many lips to be kissed, so many hands to be held and it is this holding of one another that makes us important and powerful and noticed and effective and significant and big; the darkness is dark and powerful but what you need to know and feel and dance to and dwell on with all your blessed heart is that there is poetry to be read, music to be nourished by, and person after person to be seen in all their glory and depth; there is still a whole universe of stars and fishes and birds and butterflies and waterfalls to pay attention to; there is still a multitude of good people (more than you can count) who cry over human pain and folly and do something about it every day

this is where we must look, this is where me must attend, this is our holy work, this is the only focus that brings peace

oh, dear one, can we focus on dear life, can we focus on the wonders that still abound and the fact that we can and do acknowledge our worth and the worth of every blessed one of us

look away from the darkness, look away

consider that an order

look for the light

consider that an order

i wish you peace

COINCIDENCE?

when i was a young minister i was startled awake by a grim combination of fear, guilt and terror which would have dropped me to my knees had i not been lying in bed grabbed at the throat by the fact that i apparently had said something so dumb at a funeral that the family had spoken to the undertaker about my ineptitude, which was told to me the night before by the undertaker when we went out to dinner

being of a kind disposition i do not generally like to hurt people's feelings, and being of a soft disposition, especially back then, i did not welcome the thought of people not liking everything i did because...well, you know why...it scares us more than we like to admit because we are so vulnerable, so vulnerable

lying in bed, my heart pounding, i felt the world was out to get me, but what do you do at 3 a.m. when you are alone with the night sweats?

i will tell you what i did as long as you do not forget that i know what it's like to be a little boy lying in a ditch asking god to mend my broken collarbone before daddy comes to take me to the hospital and they start setting a bone which is a pain i hope you never experience because when they set it, it seems like they could be smoking a cigarette at the same time because they are so used to setting bones that they don't notice your tears and disillusionment that not even god showed up to heal your broken body in all its beautiful little boy innocence, nor did even god warn you in the first place not to fall in that specific ditch where the old mailbox with the steel base lies waiting for your collar bone

so as long as you remember that i have my doubts, i will tell you that i decided to send an urgent prayer to heaven to help me out of my panic in the dark of the night and i even went so far as to raise my hands to the skies in hopes that i would be noticed and with all my heart and all my mind and all my soul i begged for peace and assistance

i did this quickly because my wife was lying next to me and i did not want her to know how scared i was because i did not want to know how scared i was and so i quickly said something like "god help me get out of this jam which i did not intend because all i meant to say at the funeral was how we often feel guilty that we don't visit our relatives enough in the nursing homes and that i even feel guilty as a minister not visiting people enough and even though the family took this as a direct attack i would never have meant it that way because, what would i know of that, i had never even met them before, i was just trying to talk deep and real about how hard it is to love in a busy world"

that was my prayer, whispered really fast, arms up and down really quickly, since i did not want to look or sound like a religious freak or a scaredy cat

us cool, calm collected males, brothers all are we, trying to look so tough in front of women the strangest thing happened

i felt a wave of peace come over me, as if valium was injected into my blood stream

the strangest thing happened

i fell asleep

"god help me get out of this jam"

the next morning was a sunday and my wife asked me to pick up a bottle of milk at the grocery store after i checked the heat at the church

so i am getting out of my car in the grocery store parking lot and just as i close my car door i look over at the man getting out of his car next to me and it is the head member of the family that apparently had trouble with my deep thinking

i gulp and want to get back in my car and head home to bed as i suddenly yearn for a different world than the one that apparently wants me to get out of this jam by putting on my big boy panties and going up to that man and talk things over

i look in the other direction while fear grabs me by the throat again, but i know that this opportunity is one not to be missed if i ever want to feel real peace about this incident, rather than ramming the whole thing down my already repressed and neurotic life

i catch up to the man, tap him on the shoulder and say "listen, i heard how your family viewed what i was saying at the funeral" and i explained how i meant it compared to the way they heard it and he told me, with a handshake, "bob, it took a real man to come up to me and say what you did, i will let the family know about our misunderstanding, and no hard feelings"

i never saw the man other than that day and at the funeral and i never saw him again

coincidence?

god?

who knows all the answers?

not me

but i do know this

fear is so bad, peace is so good, that only the hard-hearted and glib and facile and well off would auto-
matically knock anything that anybody does just to get a moment's peace in this at times lying in a ditch
godforsaken world

i do know this

a glass of wine on occasion, a hug, a prayer, a raising of your arms to the heavens, a bit of meditation,
talking things over, facing things, looking away from the terrible things, hoping for a heaven, a romp in
the hay, doing some charity work, doing lots of charity work, calling your friends, shedding a tear, letting a
wave of peace fill you, sleep, good coincidence

it's all good, it's real good

NO STATISTICS

what would it look like if we dedicated ourselves to the desperately needed relief of human pain, yours and others?

the look in your eyes and the thought in your brain would be different, you would see the stripper as a person, as someone's daughter, you would see the prisoner as a person, as someone's son, you would see the soldier as a person, as someone's grandson or granddaughter

you would not see statistics, you would see reality

the touch in your hand and voice would be softer, more gentle, as in judy needs your warmth she is so lonely

the touch in your hand and voice would be firmer, more insistent, as in bullets kill, as in stop the insanity, as in write a letter to the person in prison dying of loneliness

you say you can't find your purpose and don't know what to do to change the world, when all you have to do is write a letter to the person in prison dying of loneliness, all you have to do is turn off your television and call the one person you already know whose life is steeped in pain and ask "how are you?"

and then listen

you say you can't find your purpose and don't know what to do to change the world, when there is something in your life that is screamingly obvious that you need to fix, and if you take the time and courage and energy to fix that something, you will be an inspiration to the rest of us

"oh, look at her, look at what she went and did, changed herself after all these years, there's hope for the rest of us"

you must change your life

for your sake, for our sake

you will feel so good, far more peaceful, so proud

this peace movement would mean that you stop things and rearrange things and end things because the old has to go to let in the new, like they all say, but if there is going to be more peace, peace in your heart, peace in my heart, peace in the world, then there has to be action more than anything, action more than anything, not just words but words can be good, so good, so needed, words that form the thoughts that lead to peace

the stripper is way more than you think, she is a person, she is somebody's daughter, she is hurting, her life matters too

the passing of the peace to the stripper

come to think of it, this kind of thinking could actually get you a panic attack, because thoughts like this wake you to the pain, to the realness of the person you stereotype

see everyone as someone's grandchild and your life will be one of ongoing startle reflex

love leads to panic, not just peace

and then you have the peace that comes after the panic, cause you are real, engaged, in the game, not living in a gated community, not living in willful self-centered naiveté

selfishness begins and ends in panic

love begins and ends in peace

love is words and thoughts and good intention, words and thoughts all twisted into the pure potions of mercy, kindness, grace and generosity

love is action more than anything

you have to turn off your television and make the phone call, write the letter

you have to

you just have to

ELSEWHERE

peace comes when you slow down enough to realize that you are loved

someone loves you

you are accepted and held, loved like a baby in its mother's arms

peace comes when you stay with that fact, when you sit with it, when you dwell on it,

when you let it dwell in you

this takes time

all well and good

except the doubting part of you will dismiss this love in a millisecond

"you have such lovely hair"

"no, I don't"

the feeling unloved part of you will rip it to shreds

"you are so smart"

"no, my sister is far smarter and much more appreciated"

the ignored part of you won't see it

"yeah she said that about me, but i never got any money"

"it never got me laid"

the hungry part of you will move on to the next possibility for love, in the vast and varied land called "elsewhere"

"elsewhere" is that place you picture down the road where all the work is done for you—the new love will be so arresting and stunning and apocalyptic that it will throw you into a world where you don't have to do any work, as in accepting the compliment, seeing the blessing, fighting the bad mood

you have to be your elsewhere (with a little help from your friends)

you have to be your own peace maker (as in making)

you have to be your own apocalypse

the apocalypse of self-respect

SIGNIFICANCE

your frenzied search for peace

because at times you feel insignificant, so nothing compared to those who have already made it, seemingly so effortlessly, while you struggle to hold your head above the flood of crazy thoughts that pull you under

peace is knowing that comparisons are almost always destructive, a fact that my therapist, ralphie baby, yelled at me with great force in the late 80's and early 90's, and so i have known since then that no one person can reach everyone and every candle lightens some darkness

it is better to light a candle than compare

your frenzied search for peace

because you feel that you are no match for death, war, violence, and the seemingly never-ending stampede of craziness and stupidity that entertains the masses

peace comes in knowing that our loving effort is far more lovely than death and war and violence and all the stupidity

let death and war and violence and stupidity feel insecure

your frenzied search for peace

because you feel that the love given you does not outweigh all who have ignored you, hurt you, criticized you, judged you, and taken you very much for granted

peace comes when you focus only on those who love you

your frenzied search for peace

because there is so much to do, you can't even catch a breath, catch a break

who has time to soak in peace when there is so much to do?

peace comes when you dwell on your good intentions and the good you have done

peace comes when you slow down enough to know that everyone feels like a speck, from time to time, in light of all that is arrayed against us, and yet we are not specks

that we are small does not mean we are specks

in fact, we are so dazzling that many very intelligent people see us as children of the divine, wonderfully and gloriously made

STUFF

out of the corner of my eye i sneak a look at all that i own, but of course i can't see it all in a single glance

i am not ghandi

who, if i remember right, owned about ten things when he died, including the simple small bowl he ate out of every day

god bless his memory

when you possess thousands of books, hundreds of magazines, thirty two sweaters, 862 "indispens-able" items (cutlery, dishes, floss, scotch tape), a fold up christmas tree for next year, five cabinets worth of files, and enough marketing material for three lifetimes of learning, you begin to think that jesus was right when he said a man's life does not consist in the abundance of his possessions

the only possessions that do us any good are the ones we actually possess as in take care of, use, delight in, and cherish

yes, i can like my library as a whole, even if i don't get to every book, but if i took the time to look at every book i would see many that are dead to me in terms of use and delight

i should give them a proper burial

i think you will have more peace in your life if you get rid of the things that are not living to you, not living for you

it takes time to figure this out, and even more time to conduct funerals

and this requires deliberation and thinking, instead of a life swayed by the insistent pull and instant gratifications of materialism

materialism is about the crowd and what the crowd supposedly wants

deliberation and thinking is about being the individual you want to be

and what then?

a proper burial will be held for an undisclosed amount of my possessions this coming may

spring cleaning

cause of death: time and tide and neglect and clarity

how many of us are unwittingly in the storage business?

storage is a sign of our grandiosity, a space of too much, a bloated heap, a stagnant pond

peace is sane, lean, agile, limited, fresh and moving

storage is the stuffed feeling

peace is just enough

storage amasses with little discrimination

peace has a cutting edge

"this stays, that has to go"

TO HELL

peace is like everything good, you don't know what you've got till it's gone

anxiety is like everything bad, you don't know how bad bad is until it hits you

i think the only two good things about anxiety are that, in general, it warns us that we live in a dangerous world and so we better be careful, and, specifically, it alerts us to the potential rattlesnake in the bush

however, anxiety in overdrive is useless and pernicious: it has us worried about every bush, even if we're in hawaii where there are no snakes

"but maybe someone just brought in a batch of snakes on the last plane from arizona?"

as best you can, keep your worries for when you hear the rattle

and there are enough real problems that you don't need to believe the part of you that will go all imagination on you

fear is real good at imagination

let the day's own rattle be sufficient for the day

the only other good thing about anxiety is that we can, out of our anxious pain, be more alert for the presence of other people who are afraid and maybe we can join the needed crowd of people who won't go around indiscriminately hurting people because we're having a bad day or a bad life

pain is so real

people are so real

that most obvious fact that dictators and haters can't seem to fathom

blessed are the peacemakers

to hell with the fear makers

GENEROSITY

(i have a bone disease called osteogenesis imperfecta and a somewhat rare arthritis of the back called ankolosing spondylitis or bamboo spine.....this is relevant to the following)

a friend wants to know why i have gone capital-less with this series on peace and all i can say is it has helped my writing flow

another friend wants to know why i write jesus without the big j and i think it's because i am trying to make my writing about the divine less predictable, but in a world of senseless violence and cruelty and meaninglessness, i am not ashamed to say that it's not a bad idea that Jesus loves us all, that Jesus loves me this i know, loves me, loves you

i've heard worse

Jesus with the big J loves you

and what good does that do? will that bring you peace?

by and large, it can't hurt, though honestly it can

you can take the idea that Jesus loves you and twist it into self-centeredness as in Jesus and you think all alike and so now nobody can get through that thick head of yours, everything you think is divinely accurate

you can lean on Jesus when you should be going to the doctor, as in Jesus becomes your personal get out of everything card, so you don't have to think, agonize, sweat, practice, fail, and learn the ropes, do the ropes

Jesus as drug, Jesus as cop out, Jesus as a cover for my passivity

you get the picture

and, the worst case of all, where Jesus becomes my personal bully, and he hates who i hate, and so the prince of peace becomes my Godfather

see the crusades, no mission of peace there

gulp

christians all a culpa

say it ain't so

it is

i climb in bed the other day because we got a new bed and i want to see if my back is finally working, because for the past month i have been sleeping in a chair because my bamboo spine has been acting up and i have been screaming in agony when i have laid down on a massage table, chiropractor's table, x-ray machine, or my old saggy bed

the kind of screams as in the scream comes out of your mouth before you know it

the kind that grabs everybody's attention, especially me

so new bed, hope springs eternal

my hopeful experiment begins well

nice firm bed

the muscle spasms hit after about five peaceful minutes, and my body constricts in fear and my mind comes up with the conviction that i do not want to move

at all, ever

except it is 10 a.m. and i have, ironically, an appointment at the gym for a healthy back session, eventually i have to go to work, plus i can't very well write about peace for you while lying flat on my back with fear grabbing me by the throat and everywhere

my pulse quickens, my mouth goes dry, i breathe like i am in labor

and repeat, i do not want to move at all, ever, because movement means agony, or so i fear

fear and me become almost one, that is how powerful fear is

i've told you before that i sort of like these moments because they dip me deep in the river of pain and my response is to think of you and have nothing but empathy for your fear, anxiety, and possible i'm so small, insecure feelings in light of all that makes you feel alone and scared in a bed by yourself, just after you have locked the door to your house who is going to come and rescue you, rescue me?

when we can't move, because of fear

when we have locked our door

can't talk to people, can't look for a job, can't say no to our bullying spouse, can't believe we can do better, can't let our light shine

the omnipotent ones are no help as they berate us for our weakness and yell at us for letting fear get to us

the elite ones will pay us no mind, we are not uber successful, not on their radar

the have no doubt totally faith filled religious (of whatever stripe) will accuse us of unbelief

the cynical drown in their despair, helping no one, as they dismantle everything

a cackle of confident atheists are too busy with the lecture circuit to lend a sympathetic hand

oh great, thanks a lot, just what we need, more blame, dismissal and neglect

peace comes when someone meets us where we are, when we can graciously meet ourselves where we are

acceptance

understanding

it doesn't mean we don't have to move, to get out of bed, to talk to a stranger, to call an agent, to tell the bully to take a hike

it gloriously means that we are not shamed, condemned, or held in contempt, which further holds us down and stuck

the shame of stuckness

the stuckness of shame

and so, back to me in bed, so scared to move, yet knowing that i can't lay there all day as i said, me and fear are almost one, and so will you fault me if i pray to Jesus and ask for the courage to roll over, lean on my arm, push my body up, and sit on the edge of my bed longing for the happiness that comes when the pain is over?

am i wackadoodles if i yearn for loving company from possible heavenly places because, frankly, i feel alone and overwhelmed?

alone and overwhelmed

the heart of anxiety

alone and overwhelmed

the heart of why we do almost anything, from heroin to joining a book club

we are in pain, we are alone, we want relief, we want some sort of company, even if it's the drug showing up in its fast, "dependable" way

(moral discourse is the complex, honest talk about what works, in the short run, in the long run)

i bathe in pain and fear and lying there figure out for the first time, in generosity, why certain christians sort of use Jesus as a drug

it's not a cop out or a cover

they are overwhelmed and in pain

they want relief, they want to be special, as in Jesus come heal us and rescue us, so we don't have to go to the doctor and face months of physical therapy

as in send us money, huge sums of money, because for decades we have spent everything we have on anything capitalism in all its forms could seduce us to buy

as in kill our enemies, because we are terrified of their power

i am no different

when the screaming pain hits, when fear has my lips dry, i want Jesus to show up and be my heroin

i don't want to have to go through the pain....yet again

i don't want to be alone in pain...yet again

i've spent too many moments, especially as a little boy, sitting on a casting table while so used to it doctors set my bones while i screamed and cried

Jesus as heroin did not show up in my bedroom the other day, though i prayed for him or an angel to show up with a bag of tricks, and i promised that i would not give away my source

oh well

maybe there is no bag of tricks because the trick i really need is to change my life

maybe the big bag of tricks is that we be jesus for one another, and stop all the nonsense, all the needless pain, the wars, the greed, the inhumanity

if you are out on a rowboat in a massive thunderstorm, pray as if you have no oars, row as if there is no god

pray

row

it is better than beating one another with oars or capsizing one another's boats

only those who have never felt pain, or been in a storm, would make fun of anyone who prays

only those who have never felt pain, or been in a storm, would discourage anyone from learning to row

EFFORT

peace is that soft tone of voice, lined with grace, warmth, patience, understanding, and acceptance

speak to me the way you'd speak to a baby, and we'll all get along a lot better

do you have to make yourself feel better by putting someone else down? why not just flat out brag and say "i am smart" with no need to mention that you think we are dumb compared to you?

peace comes when we admit the way things are, the things we have to do, the basic structure of our life. if you have to make a living because you weren't born into money, then you probably won't have the time to read five novels a week

acceptance is hard come by, but pays dividends in terms of self-assessment and realistic judgment

blessed are the peacemakers

but notice the making part

the effort in "i am sorry"

the hard won humility of "i am mistaken"

the tearful confusion in "my way of looking at the world is 86% mistaken"

the work of starting over

certainty, arrogance, self-righteousness, the usual way—it takes such little effort

peace doesn't just float in on a cloud. we've got to make it happen.

peace is a choice, a deliberate act, a noble intention comprised of thinking, understanding, compromise, the bigger picture

blessed are the peacemakers

oh yes

NOTHING

examine anxiety and you will see and feel how much of it smears our life with a purposeless malaise that can turn everything to grey ash

who cares?

why bother?

what difference will i make?

fear chains us to our beds or chairs and seduces us to do nothing, feel nothing, stand for nothing, live for nothing, because it all feels so scary and pointless and overwhelming

"nothing" might be the devil's middle name

surely evil incarnate (whatever that is, whoever that is) wants us to lie about and do nothing while loneliness prowls our bedrooms and kitchen tables and "living" rooms as we subsist on television and crumbs of social media and don't gather for deep talk, hard work on behalf of the oppressed, delicious loving sex, or a trip to the movies

fear in your brain will spotlight all your flaws, all your confusion, the young or middle aged or old age mess you have made of things and it will urge you to give up the fight and do next to nothing

and then you will drift amidst the debris of your life and stare hopelessly at your unmade bed, your unfinished projects, the abandoned dreams that taunt you, as you see failure piled up everywhere

who warned us how hard life can be?

"what the world needs now is love sweet love, no not just for some but for everyone"

and love, above all, is action

action sweet action

do the dishes

visit one lonely relative

read a book

pay some bills

start a movie group

meditate

stretch

really kiss your partner and get things going

if you have no one to kiss, look around, explore your options of which there are several million, not everyone will reject you

make a meal for a hungry family

get moving

action is the essence of mental health

keep moving

then

nothing won't catch you

all of the above beats hatred, meanness, self-centeredness, racism, war, greed, and other human hobbies, many pleasurable for the moment, many that lead to nothingness and death

RUIN

self-control leads to peace

a substantial amount of human caution and anxiety is our brain rightly telling us "what are you thinking?" and "what on earth are you doing?"

therapy is meant to lead to self-control and assertive wisdom, which is so hard to have, and harder to implement, but so worth the effort and so vastly superior to the way in which all of us can easily drive towards a cliff or slowly build a grenade that will blow up our lives

i mean just how easy it is to self-destruct and get so used to it that we are rather calm as we point out the cliff and handle the grenade

therapy is about having someone in your corner who is appropriately alarmed at what you are doing and not crazy in the same way that you are crazy

therapy is the long, slow process of learning to trust our therapist's voice and knowing deep in our bones that we better stop listening to our stubborn, self-righteous craziness

stopping our crazy behavior can feel so dry, so moral, so pedestrian

craziness can feel like such a sexy risk, of course stimulation to a dull day

sanity can feel too safe; peace can feel too boring

and so many a couple will stay up too late and have a fight rather than go to bed and simply fall asleep

and so families will quarrel forever rather than make the weird choice to stop and listen to one another and solve a problem or two

and so an individual will drive towards the cliff because it can feel so inevitable

so inevitable because we are easily swayed by passion, driven by habit, delirious in our passivity, so blind to our illusion that hollywood or fame or money or drugs can sweeten ruin and folly

nothing sweetens ruin and folly, though "nothing" will whisper that "it's no big deal"

therapy is a place where the tears flow and ruin is seen as ruin and choice and control are viewed as better than any cliff or grenade

SOLITARY CONFINEMENT

fear works best when it places you in solitary confinement

this could be a place you are so used to, that you do not even know you are in it

and so there you will be, by yourself, sitting in a chair in front of the television, thoroughly convinced that no one wants to bother with you. you are sure that you face a scary, lonely future

or you are at your office desk, overwhelmed by all that you have to do, and you dare not share your fear that you can't handle it all, or do not know everything

and forget that you would ever dream of asking for help, for someone to share the workload

that will get you fired, you're certain of that

fear will tape your lips shut, especially if you "grew up" in a home where nothing was ever talked about

i think of those who suffer profound mental illness, like a schizophrenic whose daily life is a walking, awake nightmare, and how isolated that person is by the fact that they alone see the intense truth that the FBI is out to get them. how do you share this when no one believes you and are therefore part of the conspiracy?

yann martel in his novel, "the life of pi," speaks so rightly of fear as a "wordless darkness"

lest you under-estimate the power of fear, all you have to do is read the book called "my age of anxiety: fear, hope, dread and the search for peace of mind" by scott stossel, editor of "the atlantic magazine"

say a prayer for him, light a candle for him

most of us, including myself, have not suffered as much as mr. stossel, but i do know personally about solitary confinement

of all that i have been through lately, the worst moment for me was that night when my back was in an absorbing combination of muscle spasms and spinal nerve pain

(this pain was far worse than any pain i experienced after open heart surgery, but for most of that pain i was nicely medicated, praise be to those bright people who make that stuff)

from midnight on, every time i moved i felt like screaming

i didn't scream because my wife was sleeping beside me and i wanted her to sleep, and besides it was around christmas time and muffled screams are a nice gift to a sleeping person, don't you think?

it got to where i either could not move or would not move

i tried everything from meditation to breathing to prayer to rational cognitive therapy, but my body refused to budge, i lay in bed as stiff and still as a board

in a last desperate movie, i did what all the gurus tell you to do, i visualized something ultra-positive as a reward for getting out of bed, like you win a trip to hawaii if you simply get out of bed

i even tried the opposite. i imagined that my house was on fire, and that i had to find a phone and call 911

the best i could do was move my hand slightly, and i mean slightly

eventually, it became rather obvious that i needed help, so i broke out of my solitary confinement, woke my wife, and asked her to go find me some strong pain medicine

"i get by with a little help from my friends"

it was 4 o'clock in the morning

an hour later i got out of bed, and slept in a chair every night for almost two months

we're all so human, and an essential part of that humanity is to speak, to ask for help, to tell our fear

we're all so human, and so we afraid to speak, afraid of looking weak, afraid of rejection, afraid of shame and ridicule and embarrassment, afraid to try lest we fail

thus, an essential part of that humanity, is to be worthy of one another's vulnerability and trust

the gospel song "they'll know we are christians by our love" has in it this wonderful line: "we'll guard each man's dignity and save each man's pride"

and then we will be less afraid

there is a famous george orwell story where he was a soldier in world war one and had an opportunity early one morning to shoot an enemy combatant who did not know that orwell had him in his sights. but the man was obviously on his way to the bathroom, running in that wiggly motion when you're trying to haul up your pants and get somewhere important at the same time

orwell saw their common humanity and could not bear to pull the trigger

TAKE IT IN

someone has stopped what they were doing this past while and took notice of you

and you were so used to business as usual that you kept on doing business as usual

and you never really noticed the effort it took for them to do what they did because like the rest of us you are filled with the usual view of things that no one really cares that much or they don't really mean it or they only really bother with the others who are better than you

so you missed the effort, the attention, the peace, the love, the alternative view that was sent your way

that was in fact sent your way clearly, deliberately, and with the intent that you would stop your usual griping and wake up now to the fact that you are wanted and noticed and loved and that it would be mighty fine if you relax and don't worry so much about you and your status

CARRY WATER

there are many good things that we do each day that are part of our normal lives

we tidy up around the house, phone a friend, rake the leaves, clean out a closet, run an errand or do the dishes.

our culture overlooks the importance of these ordinary tasks and most time management experts do not remind us to put them on our "to do" list. after all, they do not seem like big ticket items of productivity and success, i think that this is misguided because a) everything that we do should be worth doing and is therefore part of our success. b) our "to do" list should calculate almost everything we do because then we have a more accurate picture of all that we have to do and we can feel more proud about what we have accomplished

when it comes to getting things done, we need all the impetus we can get. in fact, the normal, ordinary tasks are often exactly what we need to do in order to achieve peace, equilibrium, and momentum. the buddhists say:

> what should you do before enlightenment?
> chop wood and carry water.
> what should you do after enlightenment?
> chop wood and carry water.

these ordinary acts of everyday life not only keep us grounded and humble and helpful, but they are also all that we might be capable of doing at a particular time. right now you might feel tired and over-whelmed or you might be at your lowest energy point of the day. that's ok. you are human.

you are not a machine. we can't compose an Italian opera or write a magnum opus every day. if all you can do is carry water or chop wood or have a battery charging nap, that's mighty fine. the magnum opus will be much more refined after your nap. and after you have chopped some wood the creation of your opera will be blessed with a lot more energy. and who says that carrying water to a sick friend is not a magnum opus all its own?

ACCEPTANCE

anxiety. panic attacks. fear. such common words, such excruciating realities.

peace. calm. contentment. such common words, such wonderful realities and yet very under-rated until the day you get hit with a panic attack or the electric bolts of anxiety or the grey cloud of fear.

how can we have more peace?

short answer—cry more

cry for those who tell you they have panic attacks. cry when catastrophe strikes someone dear to your heart. cry when phil mickelson wins at golf for amy his wife, cry when a song touches you deeply. cry because you are happy to be alive. cry when you have been loved so well in bed that it makes you feel like a princess or a prince. cry, cry, cry

and why will this make you more peaceful? after all, it's rather strange to think so

here's the deal. when you cry, you are accepting the fact that you are human and letting that human thing happen. when we cry we are accepting our humanity. accepting our humanity will give us more peace.

"when you go to the circus, expect to see elephants"

people are built to talk. talk. tell a good listener your problems and your problems will lessen. listen to someone else's problems and you will have human company and sometimes your problems won't seem so bad

people are built to do. do. do something about your problems. don't just sit there

at times people just sit and do nothing about their problems. ok, we will give you half an hour a week to just sit there and feel sorry for yourself. we all do. accept it. half an hour. then start talking and doing and fixing

people are screwed up. it's a fact. be peaceful about the fact that you are screwed up. it's the price of admission to messy life. of course, do something about it—but don't waste too much time thinking you are the only messed up person on the block

people have been poisoned and brain-washed. we've all been given some seriously whacky viewpoints and perspectives and feelings. accept the fact that you have been poisoned. this doesn't mean "like it."

it means accept the fact. spend serious time getting your brain scrubbed and search for the anti-venom for your poison. don't spend a lot of time beating up your mother or anyone else who poisoned you. spend a lot of time finding new mothers, fresh thoughts and crystal clear, reality oriented views

people walk. go for lots of walks. it will give you peace. accept the fact that you need to move. accept the fact that you are tempted to be sedentary. finding peace is a fight. you are a soldier for peace. cry. talk. do. scrub and search. walk

people run. there are some things you should be running *from*. some things are hurting you. run, forrest, run!

people run. there are some things you should be running *to*. some things give you peace and well-being but you have forgotten them. go find them. run, forrest, run!

people need people. it's a fact. accept it. you are not co-dependent because you need people and want to have a companion or want someone to love you. there is an ocean of legitimate need inside us. attend to your needs

people hurt people. it's a fact. every close relationship is damage control and a venture in minimizing damage. be careful out there. transform your despair about people or your self-pity into shrewdness, spotting the good in the people you are close to, and being proud that you are reducing the wounds you inflict on others

people have all kinds of troubles. we have money troubles, relationship troubles, trouble at work. all of us are professionals at getting ourselves into trouble and making life difficult for ourselves. it's hard to get it all done, maybe impossible. it's hard to figure out where to go in the big picture—your dreams are not spelled out in the stars. what do I do next when there are so many options? be peaceful that life is far from a game of perfect. be peaceful about the fact that you have trouble. it is a sign you are still alive. ok, sure, you can cry about some of your troubles and you can be angry about others, but go back to that rare stance that accepts the fact that there are elephants at the circus and it is going to smell like animal

i will distinguish between "trouble" and "catastrophe". i'm not talking about profound medical illness or planes crashing or the monstrosities of violence and war. lately i have been thinking that the only things we should worry about are catastrophes, death and the fact that we might go to the grave with the music still in us. so don't be scared of playing your music—play it for you, play it for me, play it for all of us—and as you play you will remind us that we are meant to sing and dance and paint and laugh and create as much as we are meant to accept and fight the messiness of life. life can be a mess. fix it and sing.

peace is accepting facts—and then accepting that all of us, the walking, talking, doing, troubled, running and hurt people can carry on anyway because we are glad to be in the circus

AN ORDINARY DAY

as frustrating as life can be, as overwhelming as it can be, every now and then we have to stop and shout to the sky "hey, i'm alive, with goals and passion and giving it my best and fighting evil and offering the world my peace, i'm growing here and there and i've made it through many dangers , toils and snares and many people would give a million dollars for one of these too-much-to-do, can't-get-it-all done, up-to-my-eyeballs-in-obligations, i've-got my-health, hard to find a moment's peace kind of days"

lift up your head and see the big, beautiful reality called life with its salmon swimming upstream, full moons, luscious trees, and people who, like you, are looking for peace and making it happen

as i have already told you, i have a bone disease that has caused me a lot of pain. i could scientifically divide the pain up for you into three general categories—there is the sharp pain of a broken bone where you have the agony of bone on bone, the worst ever for me, being a broken femur; secondly, there is the sudden rip of muscle or tendon, which sounds like a gun going off in your head, and it leaves you speechless, because the mind can't fathom that something so devastating can happen so quickly and powerfully

these two kinds of pain have left me with a life philosophy that is very simply put: "any day you can walk to the fridge without crutches is a great day"

the third category of pain is harder to describe. it is not sharp pain, as described above, it is not dull pain like the first hint of nausea. this pain could be described as a pain of the soul, where your soul is so sick of your body pain, that you are one inch away from simply giving up, because you feel so lifeless, so beyond exhausted, so "i've just had it"

in 1998 i had my first open heart surgery for a leaky aorta valve, and my stomach stopped working after the surgery, i gained 18 lbs. of fluid in one day and felt so exhausted that i could not answer two simple questions from my kids when they came to visit me. the next morning the team of doctors came to do their rounds, they talked about me for a while and then one of the nurses interrupted them and said "we're not doing enough for this guy, he has to be utterly miserable, even though he is not complaining, and I think he will go into congestive heart failure if we don't do something"

even though i was so drained, this got my attention, and even more it got the attention of these world famous doctors who suddenly started rattling off drugs and procedures and other medical terms that apparently applied to me and the consequence was that, basically, they flushed my body of all that fluid, so that by that afternoon i felt so human again and ordinary and normal that i sat up on the edge of my bed and sobbed in relief, in utter relief

that same nurse who had basically told the doctors to "wake up and smell the roses" came in and saw me crying and she said "what's wrong?" and i looked up at her and said "nothing's wrong, i am so happy"

people of religious persuasion tell us that they are filled with god or the holy spirit and you might feel like you missed the boat. if i could tell you one thing, it would be this: if right now you are feeling healthy and nothing hurts, though you are used to this state of being, if you ever went to the lowest places, you would know that what you are feeling now is so good, so very good, that i do not think that you are mistaken at all to say that what you are feeling is divine

what you miss most when you are seriously ill is not a fancy trip or the night out on the town, but the beauty of having and getting through an ordinary day

INTERVIEW 2

HOW CAN WE RECOGNIZE WHEN WE ARE BEING STOPPED BY FEAR?

If there is an absence of creativity and fresh dreams in your life, you may be mired in routine in order to avoid facing the fear of failure. If you never step outside your circle of acquaintances and friends, you probably expect rejection. If you seldom have a quiet, open space in your life, you are probably scared of forging your own, unique journey. Or you may be scared to meet yourself and, especially, scared to meet your past, your fears, and whatever despair you live in believing "it's too late" or "I'm hopeless".

Of course, there are certain kinds of fear that are alarming, terrifying, and all too obvious in an (at times) violent, cruel and harmful world. I will not go into what it must be like to have a gun pointed at your head, see a rattlesnake in your path, or know you are sitting on a plane with failing engines. My clients trust me because I do not shy away from the fact that there are plenty of reasons we should be afraid. And I never promise anything that guarantees a safe world or that something will turn out well. We live in a world of probability, not certainty. All we can hope for in ourselves is reasonable calm and the ability to see what is happening in front of us. And that is a gift, a hard earned praxis, or some combination thereof.

However, the most common fear is the fear that does not announce itself at all. You could be sitting at your desk daydreaming about your upcoming speech and fear will not usually announce "You are petrified about this speech, start flipping through the television channels." Fear can be like carbon monoxide in that it silently makes its move and compels us to take a safer route, to avoid what scares us, even though we do not know we are scared.

SINCE ANXIETY IS SO POWERFUL, DO YOU OFTEN FEEL POWERLESS WHILE YOU WORK WITH CLIENTS?

About twenty years ago one of my clients was in a psychiatric ward because he was getting off of massive rounds of alcohol and Xanax and he was in an overwhelming state of fear. I didn't feel as hopeful in helping him as I tried to sound. But I remembered a bit of Shakespeare and quoted it to him:

Polonius: To be mad (crazy), tis to be all mad?
Hamlet: No, I am but mad, north northwest
              When the wind blows southerly, I can tell
              A hawk from a handsaw.

I more than wondered if it would do any good. But he understood, and later told me that the moment changed his life because the truth of those words gave him hope. He saw that his fear was only a part of him, and not the whole self, and that the winds of his life would change.

This moment taught me an oft repeated lesson too. None of us are as brave as we look, but we would be a lot braver if we knew what a difference our words and actions make in the lives of other people.

The more I have practiced psychotherapy, the more I have seen the power of anxiety. Fear-ridden children and teenagers can get so used to their way of being that they don't really notice their unease until they become adults. By then, the pathways of anxiety are well in place and solid as rock. People usually under-estimate both the power of fear and all the work that necessary to lessen fear. There are no "Ten Easy Steps to Conquer any Fear!"

IN YOUR WRITING YOU STRESS ACTION AS MUCH AN ANYTHING. CAN YOU EXPLAIN THAT FACT, GIVEN THAT THERAPY IS SO MUCH ABOUT WORDS?

I can best answer with the old Buddhist story. All the monks line up outside a certain room and are told that if they walk from one side of the room and through the door on the other side of the room, they will experience Nirvana. But they are also told they will experience all the fears they have ever felt in their whole life while they are in that room. Their Zen master tells them that this will be very scary and they will not all make it. To help you, he told them, I will offer you two golden truths: 1) remember that all the fears you are experiencing are only in your head 2) no matter what happens or what you feel, just keep putting one foot in front of the other and walk across the room.

All the monks who made it to Nirvana told their Master that the first truth did not help them because the fears were so real and powerful. The only thing that got them to the door was putting one foot in front of the other.

In this story it is words that give guidance and truth, but it is the action that makes the biggest difference. Fear keeps us in place, and that place casts a spell on us, and we need to run from that place, to shake off the spell.

CAN YOU MENTION A FEW BOOKS THAT CAN HELP US FIND MORE PEACE?

David Allen's *Getting Things Done: The Art of Stress Free Productivity* is a book that I would claim as indispensable in managing the overwhelming nature of modern life. The best introduction to GTD that I have read is "Organize Your Life" by James Fallows, Atlantic Magazine July/August 2004.

Frederick Buechner is a widely esteemed writer of spiritual truth whose books have been a source of peace for many. I especially recommend *The Sacred Journey*, *Eyes of the Heart*, and *Telling the Truth*.

James Gustafson *Self-Delight in a Harsh World* (W.W. Norton & Co. New York, NY. 1992) is the work of a psychiatrist who seems to have read everything and he offers deep perspectives from political theory, history, English literature, and his own field.

Dom Bede Griffith's *The Golden String*—the spiritual autobiography of one of C.S. Lewis' students.

The poetry of Mary Oliver.

The War of Art by Stephen Pressfield is a modern, much heralded classic about battling resistance as we attempt to produce art, including the art of a life well lived.

Women Food and God: An Unexpected Path to Almost Everything by Geneen Roth. It evokes holiness in the best sense of the word. Anne Lamott says this book "will free untold women from the tyranny of fear and hopelessness around their bodies."

Wilfrid Sheed *In Love With Daylight: a Memoir of Recovery* (Simon & Schuster, New York, NY. 1995) Mr. Sheed makes sobriety sound more appealing than any other writer I know. He is funny and wise.

And I must mention Rumi Rilke's *Letters to a Poet*, the chapter "Delight in Order" in *How To Do Things Right: The Revelations of a Fussy Man* by L. Rust Hills; Thomas Kelley *A Testament of Devotion*; Donald Hall *LifeWork*; Barbara Brown Taylor *Leaving Church: A Memoir of Faith*; "On Being a Self Forever" in *Self-Consciousness: Memoirs* by John Updike; Iris Murdoch's *The Sovereignty of Good*; the book on golf and spirituality called *Golf in the Kingdom* (now out as a movie); *The Wind in the Willows*, by Kenneth Grahame; *The No. 1 Ladies' Detective Agency* series by Alexander McCall Smith; *Gilead* by Marilynne Robinson; Anne Lamott's *Bird by Bird*; *Tao te Ching* (translated by Stephen Mitchell); M. Scott Peck *The Road Less Travelled*—all of these, most elegant and poignant and unique, peace inducing in their own way.

ANY FINAL WORDS?

My deepest gratitude, once again, to the entire team of medical professionals who saved my life, and the host of relatives and friends, colleagues and clients who showed me much love. Who can repay such a gift, such love?   This book is a sign of my gratitude.

Peace be with you.

CONTRIBUTORS

BOB BEVERLEY is a psychotherapist with and Co-Director of Northeast Counseling Center in the mid-Hudson valley of New York State, USA. He has written *Emotional Elegance* (with a preface by David Allen, author of *Getting Things Done*); *Dear Tiger: A Book for Tiger Woods and for Us All*; *How to Be a Christian and Still Be Sane*; and *The Secret Behind the Secret Law of Attraction* (with Kevin Hogan, Dave Lakhani, and Blair Warren). Bob is available for motivational speaking, consultation, and psychotherapy. Bob is also the leader of a unique, life-changing experience called THE M GROUP which takes place at Mohonk Mountain House, New Paltz, N.Y.

He is a native of New Brunswick, Canada. He graduated with a degree in philosophy and English Literature from Gordon College, Wenham, Mass. He spent a junior year abroad at the University of Edinburgh in Scotland. He received a Masters of Divinity from Princeton Theological Seminary. Bob received a Certificate in Psychotherapy and Marriage and Family Therapy from the Blanton-Peale Graduate Institute in New York City in 1991. To learn more about Bob Beverley, please visit his web sites: www.findwisdomnow.com or www.emotionalelegance.com

DAVID SPAGNOLO is a New York Metro based Fashion/Beauty/Sports Advertising Photographer. For 30 years he has shot Fashion for the biggest Retailers; Portraits for Grammy, Tony and Academy Award winners, most recently focusing on sports as Art, covering NBA, MLB, and Boxing. David can be reached through his website at www.davidspagnolo.com

JULIE SPAGNOLO is an Artist, Nature Photographer and Art Educator. Julie has a degree in Graphic Art and Design and worked as a fashion art director for many years. Inspired by the beauty, color, art and design of nature she documents what she sees in everyday life. View her work on Instagram @Juliespag

MARIAN GRUDKO is a composer, writer, storyteller and editor who lives in the Hudson Valley of New York State. "Come What May" is an excerpt from "Dragonfly Bog," her musical tale of an endangered wetland and the creatures who live there. "You Are Enough" is a love song, dedicated to all who have lived through pain. Marian can be reached at mariangrudko@gmail.com, and at her website, mariangrudko.com.